You don't have to be a genius.....

You don't have to be a genius.....

Biography of a medical student/doctor in London at the dawn of the permissive age

Diana Ashworth

Clinical Press Ltd (Bristol UK)

A catalogue record for this book is available from the British Library

ISBN 978-1-85-457108-3
You don't have to be a genius...
© Diana Ashworth 2022

Published by:
Clinical Press Ltd.
Redland Green Farm, Redland, Bristol, BS6 7HF

Introduction

Readers like to know where they are with a biography. Is this real or is it fiction? If only it were that simple!

This is autobiographical, it recounts the formative events of my life, many of which happened over fifty years ago. The reason I remember them is because they changed the way I look at the world – I have thought about them repeatedly over the years and this reimagining, which is after all what memory is, probably involved some editing.

A friend tells me that she has heard the joke I remember making in 1965 in lots of other places. I thought it was mine and maybe it was and has gone around the world twice since I made it… Or maybe not. This sneaking doubt about the reliability of memory has made me change the names of most of the individuals and the locations in this memoir – to remind you that these are now the people and places in my imagination.

At times I felt that a person I remembered deserved their own voice, these sections are fictional, or second hand, and written in italics.

I make no apology for the casual sexism of my account. These were the days when the nomenclature of the medical profession was still male, doctors were assumed to be men unless specified otherwise and juniors were all housemen, regardless of gender. To call someone a 'lady' or a 'gentleman' rarely referred to their class – it reflected the good manners of the speaker and respect for the person described.

Medicine seems to have grown and changed out of all recognition, this is a glimpse of the way it was.

Diana Ashworth
2021

Acknowledgements

I would like to thank Peter Carr, Marie-Noelle, and other friends and family who helped me prepare this manuscript.

Chapter 1

DAWN OF THE PERMISSIVE SOCIETY
'You don't have to be a genius to be a doctor.'

That's what set me off – it was said by a tall, wizened old doctor, sitting opposite me, behind a child's school desk, like something from Alice in Wonderland. It was at a careers convention, I was in my early teens and my mother sat next to me smiling encouragingly at us both.

Evidently you just had to jump through the various hoops. (I was good at obstacle races.)

This was a new concept – the view had always been promoted that in fact the contrary was true. Extreme cleverness and Latin were required to practice any profitable profession (the law, medicine and the Church) – mystique and magic jargon were obligatory.

This was a unique time – a little window of opportunity. I was born in 1950, into a society underpinned by the notion of life-long monogamy and austerity; all of a sudden, under the weight, perhaps, of the post-war population bulge, all this would subside... But not quite yet.

First there was a short interlude, a golden age, of frugal diet and good education, an era when information (limited by printing capacity) was heavily edited, compacted, accessible and reasonably reliable – when one man, or woman, could pretty well grasp everything that they needed to do their job and live their life. These were the days when a family solicitor knew the law – one wig fits all. The family doctor might whip out your appendix or your gall bladder, deliver your baby (maybe even get it adopted) and treat any medical condition himself (or even herself). If you were the borough engineer or a hospital secretary or a bank manager, you'd have a pretty good idea of what was going on around you so there was less risk of you plummeting down a crevasse, into something outside your comfort zone – beyond your area of expertise.

You didn't have to be a genius to practice medicine! So, I returned to my girls' grammar school with this valuable information and listened very carefully to what my teachers said, and I asked a lot of irritating questions because, if nothing else, I was always inquisitive. I smiled with unbounded pleasure when an answer satisfied my curiosity, but I fear a shadow would cross my expressive face when I detected uncertainty or dismissiveness in the answer. This did not endear me to the didactic and, I thought, rather silly geography teacher: the one with the flouncy walk and the flattened bun atop her substantial frame which wobbled precariously as she flounced. Geography gave me up, which was just as well as, strangely, nobody did very well in Geography at that time.

My unconscious expressiveness, and a parallel receptiveness to the non-verbal utterances of others would always be a mixed blessing. It could certainly promote empathy but sometimes betrayed thoughts best censored, it would get me into trouble. It would create bonds with the most unlikely people but could also make me enemies.

Another talent that would impact on my future was my dyslexia – another mixed blessing – not admitted to anyone for many years. This was a secret shame though hardly recognised by anyone at the time and, to be fair, it did not seem to hold me back. It caused me grief and made me funnier than I might have been. Humour was my only protection, it was the distraction that I wielded when threatened with reading aloud. I developed comedy routines around mislaying or dropping or breaking my glasses and bizarre speech disorders associated with new dental braces (ones I never wore at any other time as witnessed by my front teeth to this day). I can imagine the head of English counselling the probationary teacher, 'Just don't ask Diana Grant to read – she's the scruffy one who sits at the front right-hand corner, always twisted round to see the faces of the other girls – she'll be as good as gold if you leave her alone. Try to make her read and you'll have a pantomime!'

However, by and large they did leave me alone and I did alright, I hopped through their hoops.

Although, as everyone knows, sexual intercourse began in 1963 – late for Philip Larkin, it was just about right for me. It meant I knew it was coming and had time to prepare and ask a lot more questions.

In the following year, 1964, an exquisite looking girl, in the year below, tall, slim and elegant with a cream complexion and hair the colour of egg-custard left the school suddenly and under a mysterious cloud. She had been seen the day before dishevelled and with strange bruises on her face and neck. Nobody knew exactly what had happened, but it was assumed that the poor girl had in some way fallen victim of her own undoubted sexual charisma. She was never seen again.

While my peer group were engaged in crushes on pretty teachers (who did not teach Geography), I was flirting outrageously with the beautiful sixth-form boy from the Tech in the safety of the school bus. He enjoyed the attention but did not respond, otherwise the whole course of this history could have been very different.

I must explain that my grammar school was new, not just to me but also to the world and to Miss Hasslingdon, the headmistress, enjoying her first appointment as such. It had been primed with a few girls whisked from the jaws of a recently dissolved, experimental comprehensive school (it hadn't worked the first time) but the first intake of its very own was mine. M.H. (Mary Hasslingdon) had travelled around all the junior schools and interviewed all the applicants, she was from Lancashire, unfamiliar with the geography or the social mores of the Home Counties, therefore unable to make her choices according to the address of the applicant (a process made simpler some years later by the introduction of post-codes). She made all her choices personally.

One evening, on the way home from school, I and several of my friends were involved in a high spirited but good-humoured brawl on the top deck of the bus. Some younger boys from the Tech had taken my beret hostage (it was the most expensive item of the school uniform, made in six sections or royal blue cloth, sewn into a wide band and trimmed with gold and scarlet twisted cord with a red and gold embroidered badge and had been chosen in a moment of uncharacteristic pride by Miss Hasslingdon shortly after she'd attended a meeting at one of the grander girls' public schools. It epitomised all her hopes for the new enterprise. When the bus reached our stop there was an avalanche of blue clad squealing girls down the steps at the rear of the vehicle followed moments later, as the bus resumed its onward journey, by myself, recognised by the relief French teacher travelling below as I leapt off the moving vehicle – sans-beret. The splendid object, icon of opportunity and feminist values, was ejected from the rear window of the bus and landed on top of the concrete bus shelter, where it settled to taunt exclusivity and where its ghost remains to this day.

Having had an inquest into the loss of my regulation school beret, thrown from a window of the upper deck of said bus by an unidentified boy from the Tech, and after pressure had been applied by several of her prettier and younger, married teachers, fed up with being stalked by third form girls[1], the head mistress decided that her pupils should be introduced to the concept of social interaction with the other half of the world in a more controlled environment than a lurching green bus. There was to be a school dance for the dissipation of inappropriate sexual energy.

This was probably not altogether wise and may have been the beginning of the decline but, in mitigation, it was preceded by several seminars about relationships and a visit from a lady from the Family Planning Association, but only to talk to those girls planning to leave school at fifteen which insulted them and infuriated the others.

Boys were invited through the agencies of several enterprising mothers who knew other mothers who had boys. Although brothers seemed reluctant to get involved, their friends, when they heard about it, urged them to co-operate. Thus, in a miasma of 'Old Spice' and to music from the Beatles the slippery slide to complete social havoc was begun at the first school dance (circa 1964), and very fine it was too!

I found that boys smelled nice and that I quite liked kissing some of them (not all, and one at a time). One in particular seemed to enjoy kissing me. We were not alone in this and private fixtures were arranged, mainly at the cinema but also at parties in private houses. Oddly, and probably because it was strange and new, and we were not prompted by constant sexual imagery – for several years nothing progressed much beyond kissing. Advertising agencies had not yet worked out that everything from engine oil to sanitary towels had to be sexy. Perhaps it was just a lack of imagination – it was as if a whole generation needed to relish the experience. For academic girls and boys living with parents and with virtually no disposable income of our own, so of no interest to the media, the rules of engagement were strict. It was a gentle, sensual interlude without angst – a whole

1) *Now known as year 9.*

10

generation engaged in a prolonged, delicious period of relatively innocent fore-play – another golden age.

I had decided that, until my future was secure, and I had progressed far enough to be able to deal with any consequence of my actions, my legs would remain bolted together at the knees; a wise move as contraception that was considered fool-proof did not become generally available until 1967.

Mary Hasslingdon was one of a dying breed of dedicated, selfless women with a vocation – women who foreswore marriage and children of their own to bring up or to educate other women's offspring. They were the Matrons and Mothers Superior giving up everything for their careers and for the greater good. Okay, some had their issues. Others just didn't feel the need – who cares about that? Miss Hasslingdon was a Christian.

She had a sense of humour: 'Diana, when future assaults are made upon your, soon to be replaced, beret, as well they might, it is essential that you conduct yourself more decorously. Do you understand?'

I stood next to my friend Jane before Miss H's huge desk, the other girls known to travel on the A303, 3:35 pm bus from the town centre arrayed behind us. Our heads were bowed in shame, theirs in the hope of anonymity. I looked up at the headmistress and, after a tiny tell-tail hesitation, I nodded.

'Now, go straight from here to the library and look up the word *decorously.*'

Behind us there was an unseemly scramble for the door. Jane, my closest friend, and I said, in unison 'Thank you Miss Hasslingdon.' Miss H nodded almost imperceptibly, and we turned deliberately towards the door and left.

Outside the others were nowhere to be seen. We walked briskly to the library.

'*Pertaining to decorum,*' read I, 'that doesn't help much!'

'Look up *decorum!*'

'*Behaviour in keeping with good taste and decency.*'

'Both very subjective,' said Jane, who was clever.'

'*Subclavian… Subjacent… Subject… Subjective: Relating to the subject,*' read I. '*Derived from, expressive of, existing in, one's own*

11

consciousness, what does that mean, Jane?'

'It means everyone has their own idea of what's good and what's bad.'

'That's alright then, isn't it – we're allowed our own idea of, what was it… "Good taste and decency".'

That is how I learned the power of education and of the written word, how, with the help of my friend Jane, I started to work out the world – but it wasn't without its dangers.

*

'Mum!' I said.

'Yes, Darling.'

'What, exactly, do homosexuals do?' It was a year or so later and there was much discussion in the media about the Homosexual Reform Bill (I'm sure that wasn't exactly what it was called).

'I'm not actually sure, I asked your father once, but he wouldn't tell me.'

'We need a book, Mum.' So, the following week when we were on holiday in Cornwall, we found a bookshop and browsed the blue Pelican paperbacks – they had blue covers, not because the contents were in the least bit salacious. In fact, they were very dry. We found one entitled 'Homosexuality'. It didn't help much, but it had a bibliography. I copied out the references for a likely looking book and made haste to the library where my request card appeared to provoke panic in the lady librarian. Actual *panic attacks* had not been invented – this may be the very first one recorded. She blanched and hyperventilated, fanned herself with the offending card and called weakly for the senior librarian, one of those professionals that I mentioned who understood all the nuances of his trade.

'Are you over twenty-one?'

'No.'

'This book is only available to someone who is over twenty-one.'

'My mum is over twenty-one, it's for her.' I said.

'Then she'll have to order it herself, in person.'

Two hours later I presented my mother to the senior librarian who graciously accepted the very same request card which was duly processed.

'We will let you know by post when the volume has arrived.'

'Lovely,' said Mum, 'can Diana pick it up.'

'Oh, I'm afraid not, Madam, it's on a list of strictly proscribed publications. You will have to pick it up in person and sign for it.'

A week later, when I got home from school, Mum was missing, as was her bike but there was a scribbled note, 'Gone to Library.'

I set off on my bike to meet her. As I rounded the bend of our tree lined road a figure on a bicycle, wobbling precariously, could be seen in the distance, struggling towards me. In the wicker basket attached to her handlebars was a huge tome. A second volume was hung in a cloth bag from the handlebars and was dragging the rider into the gutter. They were the biggest books I had ever seen and quite unsuitable for anyone on a bicycle (let alone a minor, under twenty-one!). I relieved her of the swinging volume of 'Sexual Behaviour in the Human Male (1948), by Kinsey et al, and together we cycled home, strangely unbalanced by the sheer weight of indecency. It was laid on the dining room table (as indeed had some of the respondents to its exhaustive study into male sexuality). Mum and I studied it at length. It was a fairly straight-forward scientific analysis of the infinite variety of the sexual proclivities and tastes (very subjective) of the American male. 'Your Auntie Gertie always liked Americans,' said Mum.

Thus, in less than a week I had, with my slow but retentive reading, consumed and processed the entire output from several years' work of an eminent US scientific institution and several PhDs – sexual curiosity is a powerful motivator, and I had achieved all this at no cost to myself and without contracting any venereal disease or becoming pregnant!

Armed with these incredible insights I soon became the font of all knowledge on sexual matters. When deliberating on the subject of bestiality one of my friends was heard to ask, rhetorically, 'Uch! How low can you get?'

'A Jack Russell terrier, I think.' I said without hesitation.

Now the problem was that, though possessed of encyclopaedic knowledge, I had scant practical experience so that when the subject of Free Love was raised in the sixth form common room, to which we had just been admitted, I was out of my depth, although I didn't know it at the time.

With adequate, reliable contraception I could see no practical objection to Free Love, in fact it seemed rather a good idea. My friends, who also had absolutely no idea of what they were talking about, concurred. One quiet girl was listening carefully to all this. She had slightly more grasp of the complexity and practicalities of the subject as she was being put under pressure by a truanting boy that she had met at the public playing field. He was an attractive young man but from a very different background and with very different aspirations from our peer group. However, as I had explained it, everything seemed quite straight forward, and the quiet girl felt reassured. A little later, like the girl with custard coloured hair, the quiet girl disappeared.

Now it is strange how we can accept the sudden disappearance of a person who inexplicably drops out of a context. One explains it to oneself – she's got a cold or she's late with her history homework. As the time goes on and discussions ensue it may be considered that she had examination nerves, or she's had a nervous breakdown (whatever that is) or that the family were short of money and that she needed to get a job. The strange thing was that, in this case, nobody went round to her house to find out. She just dropped out. That's what we say and that is what it's like and it shouldn't be, should it? She was a friend! We had an inkling of the truth, that group of friends and a sneaking misgiving that we may have played an indirect part in our friends imagined fall from grace. It wasn't that she was irrevocably damaged, I found that out decades later, more that she had plunged headlong into something she did not understand and when she came up for air, the victim of a young man, though younger than herself, who felt the need to control her, she was changed. She was so changed that there was no going back. She was a cautionary tale – a sacrifice on the altar of opinionated claptrap.

Looking back, I find little excuse for dispensing such rash advice about Free Love. I myself, at a crucial time, had received the correct advice and had remembered for my own circumstances but viewed the rest of the world differently. At the age of thirteen or fourteen (maybe even younger), when my own personal hormones were doing extraordinary things to my body, I was in the habit of visiting the swimming pool. It was out of doors and unheated so normally very quiet. During these visits I'd wrap a large towel around my shoulders and talk to Bruce, the lifeguard.

Bruce was eleven years my senior, you can do the maths. He was a small, slim, very muscular man with an even, occupational tan the colour of foxes and dead bracken and with a line of intriguing hair, like fine gold threads extending from the top of his tiny, bulging trunks, converging to a thin line and disappearing, tidily, into his tummy button. He had short cropped blond hair and was not handsome, but he chatted to me when it was quiet and he listened to what I said and commented on what was happening to my body in a very matter of fact but appreciative way. The side of the pool was raised into a small catwalk along which Bruce strutted back and forth occasionally stopping to look carefully at someone holding their breath under water, to make sure they were not dead, or to shout at little boys doing bombshells too close to the diving boards. Bruce was a good, conscientious lifeguard.

'You are getting a very tasty body,' he said when I presented myself for his approval in my new bikini, 'very tasty, you'll be driving those young lads wild – you'd better be careful. A body like that is like a loaded pistol – it has to be handled very carefully.'

I laughed.

Bruce did not. 'It's like a beautifully tuned instrument and you have to learn how to play it properly. You start with the basics and build up gradually and keep away from the older lads until you know what you are doing. Do you understand what I'm saying?'

'Not really. Why do people talk in riddles when they mention sex? My mum's always saying give them an inch and they will take a mile – I don't know what she's on about either.'

'Young men like those locker-room boys. I hear them talking. They'll tell a young girl like you whatever she wants to hear to wheedle their way into her knickers –you do know the facts of life, don't you?'

'Of course, I do – we did it in biology.'

'Well, there's more to it than what you learn in biology – that body of yours has got its own agenda – you know what an agenda is?' I nodded, 'Mother Nature doesn't necessarily want what you want for yourself and she knows how to mess with your feelings and your brain. Before you know it you'll be saying and doing things best left unsaid and undone… Your body's job is to find a mate and have babies – whether you want to or not! Remember that.'

This dialogue went on, on and off, for a couple of summers. Anyone looking from the other side of the pool with cynical eyes might have thought that Bruce was doing what men do and biding his time until I was older, what they now call grooming. In fact, he was doing the opposite.

Anyway, by the time I was older, Bruce had gone. From being someone in my fantasies every night, he became another person who just dropped out of my life. Someone said he might have gone to college.

Just before I left school, the senior swimming team went to an inter-school match and I recognised (with difficulty) the un-bronzed, un-bleached and clothed form of Bruce accompanying another team. I asked who he was and was told he was their new student teacher.

'Good,' I thought, 'he'll be good at that!'

One does not know whether Miss Hasslingdon wrestled with the issues of human sexuality that would threaten her girls in the coming world – the issues that one might assume she had managed to side-step herself. Already situations had arisen that had called for experience and competence that despite her undoubted vocation, she just didn't have.

Chapter 2.

If the Girl with Custard Coloured Hair could speak for herself:

'*I* can remember the exact moment that it all changed – I thought 'No – I am going to school!'

It was my life; that was what I did – I went to school. What they did at home was something else.

But it was a big mistake. That bitch, Hasslingdon, had to stick her big nose in, and before I knew it she's feeding me Jaffa Cakes in that office of hers and we're waiting for the woman from the social services and she's wittering on about 'is she her brother's keeper' or something.

It wasn't as if anything very different had happened – it had all been going on since I was eleven – the only thing that had happened was that Mam had found out and found out when she'd had a skin-full and she beat the shit out of me. It was a shame though, because that school was alright. There were a few stuck-up bitches but generally you got respect and an education would have been useful.

Once I'd climbed out of that window I never went back to that house. They whisked me off to a place of safety – that was a joke. Leched after by fat, ugly strangers instead of my mum's boyfriend, the brother of my dad (who I can't hardly remember and who should have looked after me and kept me safe). And the do-good women who judged me and got off on what I was telling them because I thought it might help to tell someone. I could see them pleased with themselves at first, thinking how broadminded and unshockable they were, but then I saw them thinking that I must be some sort of nymphomaniac and all the time they are wishing it was them because they understood nothing. In the end I told them what they wanted to hear, to get it over with, because they told me it would help... But nothing helps. I was still a dirty bitch and not just at home now. I was 'in care' and the only ones who wanted me under their roof had got their own disgusting plans for me. Nobody wanted me in their happy home with proper mums and dads and brothers and sisters because nobody wanted me seducing their husband or giving their son the clap.'

Chapter 3.

Marriage Guidance

At about this time a man joined the staff of the girls' grammar school. The art master had been a man for a long time, but he didn't really count as he spent so much of his time locked in the stock cupboard, mainly with the key turned from the inside and occasionally from the outside. He suffered sexual harassment which one must assume was preferable to the non-sexual harassment that he had suffered previously in a mixed comprehensive school. Anyway, he stayed for many years.

The new master, Walter MacTafferty, taught Chemistry and was a very different kettle of fish. In those days, before the explosion in scientific research, Chemistry was fairly straight forward and clearly delineated, even at 'A' level, and given a group that was well motivated and had a decent textbook, the nitty-gritty could be left to the students so the class-time could be spent answering their questions (he did know his subject) and exploring his real interest.

MacTafferty had recently trained as a Marriage Guidance Counsellor and had read widely on the subject of sexual relationships. He was exactly what this cohort of girls needed, although we didn't realise it at the time. He was very frank and uninhibited, and he was a man, albeit an elderly man (to us girls, at any rate). He helped dispel many of our misconceived notions about the opposite sex. Years later I would be amused but sad when my friend (not from my school) who was training to be a psychosexual counsellor explained why her study group contained no men – they were beyond the pale, impossible, there had only been two in the first place but we had to ask them to leave – they were obstructive and you just couldn't reason with them, they took such a different view from the rest of the group. Mr MacTafferty knew all about this syndrome – he and his wife had discussed it at length.

One of the girls in my Chemistry class was Chrissie – she was the most extrovert, lively and sporty girl in our class, with short cropped golden hair that shimmered with perpetual, good-humoured movement – we all loved her. One day Chrissie was absent then the next (she never usually missed a day). After a week or so she re-appeared during the afternoon, pale and faded – she had trouble at home. She was seen in the Chemistry prep-room drinking tea with Mr MacTafferty. It was near to the end of the 'A' level courses and we had a lot of flexibility and could come and go pretty well as we liked, provided we told the school secretary if we went out. Chrissie had left home (she had never got on with her mother – that was all that was said). She found digs in a council flat on the bypass with a widowed colleague of Mrs MacTafferty (Chrissie was the most popular girl in the year but she didn't stay with a friend – nobody asked her). Chrissie attended when she could – perhaps she had a part-time job, and she took her exams and passed and went to university.

Although we grumbled that Walter MacTafferty never taught us any Chemistry, the chemistry he was explaining would be much more relevant to our futures. We all passed with good grades and although none of us could tell you now exactly what was discussed in that exhaustive 'A' level course, none of us would accept violence within a relationship or think that it was our fault. None of us would be as surprised as we might have been when our husbands were unfaithful, or our daughter announced that she was in love with another woman, or if the people who were supposed to love us let us down. We had always known it was a possibility.

We understood that we would not own our children, that we are all made differently and that our marital home (however much we had contributed to it) would not belong exclusively to us – we wouldn't rush into divorce blindly. We knew that we could only control ourselves, that we couldn't stop other people from falling in love or dying, or leaving, but if they did, we didn't have to follow a stereotyped emotional path – we could use our brains and limit the damage to our own personalities and to the people we loved.

Chapter 4.

The Secret Service

In March 1968 something happened in England. It was a time of political awakening in the generation that had been born after the War. It was happening in France too. Students wanted a say. My French friend and pen-pal, Mireille, would be manning the Paris barricades by May.

For my friends and I, it all started with a vague humanitarian concern for the poor people that were caught up in the war in Vietnam. There had been a lot on the News – pictures of children napalmed – napalm was something flaming, sticky and horribly toxic that the US chucked out of planes. We talked about it in our United Nations Youth Group and agreed – something should be done. We settled on a rally, in our little town. It was to collect money for medical aid and to increase awareness of the plight of... Etc... Etc.

Most of us were still at school so the date was set for April the 15th – Easter Monday (we could have an Easter bonnet competition and parade, sell cakes and garden flowers – there would be races, whack-the-rat and maybe a slippery pole). It was 10th of March so we had 5 weeks to get ourselves organised. There was no time to lose – our chairman wrote immediately to the local paper announcing our plan and we all felt very pleased with ourselves.

The day that the Editor opened the letter (he didn't get many) was the day of the Grosvenor Square Riot in London.

This was a protest against the war in Vietnam that had started peacefully enough in Trafalgar Square. They had then marched to the United States Embassy in Grosvenor Square where it had got out of hand – punches were thrown, stars and striped were burned, policemen's helmets were knocked off and young men and women with long hair were carted away in Black Marias. Nothing like it had been seen for decades... 'And it is all about to kick off here, in this sleepy little town in a month time – are we to allow this?' wrote the Editor.

The paper asked Lawrence Smout, a Tory Councillor for his comments. *'I'm asking the Prime Minister to call up the reserves. We need the militia to deal with these lawless rioters and Communist sympathisers. The proposed rally here must be banned and riot police with water cannon in place to defend the peace of our streets.'*

'A water cannon certainly trumps a slippery pole,' said Jane as we hastily convened an extraordinary meeting to discuss the recent publicity. The chairman was not amused – he had ambitions in the Young Liberals and planned to stand as a Liberal councillor.

'Surely, if we make it clear that we are only collecting for humanitarian aid and that we aren't Communists and that we won't be sending it to the Viet Cong, it should be alright,' I said weakly.

'Smout is slippery. I've crossed swords with him in the past, and he has the ear of the local press – he'll make political capital out of it whatever we say. The trouble is – everyone has their own agenda.'

We agreed for lots of different reasons that events had overtaken us, and the Vietnam War Rally Sub-committee was dissolved and all plans abandoned.

This in itself was an enormous lesson in the uncontrollability of events – of the unpredictability of the destination once you set a ball in motion – you bowl it off with your chosen vector, it hits an unseen molehill, or more likely, someone else's boot and before you know it you have started World War III.

A week later there was a knock at our front door. It was a handsome young policeman in plain clothes, a sergeant from Special Branch. He was ushered into our chilly, polish scented, dining-room where he talked to Dad. I sat on the stairs opposite the dining room door but all I could hear was the drone of my father's voice, I couldn't make out what was being said. Mother (good in a crisis) having nothing to offer the secret policeman, had rushed to the kitchen to make a batch of drop scones.

Soon, Dad opened the door, he smiled reassuringly, which in itself was scary, and asked me to join them. I sat next to my father at the dining-room table opposite the police officer – I, it seemed, was the object of his interest. He asked a lot of questions – my age, education, my friends and my plans.

I had come to their notice because of my membership of a committee involved in recent plans to hold an anti-war rally ... Not an anti-war rally – I explained that in our naiveté we had only planned to collect for the victims of the war. None of us were politically active (well, the chairman was a Liberal, but that doesn't count, does it?) We had just felt sorry for the poor, burned children. 'It was a can of worms and it blew up in our faces.' The hint of a smile crossed the sergeant's face – he was a literal sort of chap.

He reassured my father and I that he was confident that I was not in any way subversive myself but, in view of my recent activities, I might become a recruitment target of those who might be. He would like me to 'keep in touch' and tell him if anyone did make an approach. I could 'go along with them' for a bit if I liked, provided I reported back on what they were up to.

'Oh, I wouldn't want to do that. I've already had my fingers burned once,' I said, throwing in another metaphor for good measure.

'That is entirely up to you, but your information would be very useful to us and we would appreciate it.'

There was a knock and a pretty head appeared around the door, 'can I bring you some coffee, and a few scotch pancakes?'

Oh, lovely,' said the sergeant, 'just what I need – we're all finished now. Thank you, Mrs Grant.'

Later Mr Grant, who rarely spoke on serious matters, pointed out to me that I was on the radar of the intelligence services. Indeed, it seemed that they were interested in recruiting my services in a part-time capacity – not bad at seventeen he might have thought, but he did not say. He told me to keep my ears open, my mind open and, where possible, my mouth shut, and never to join any political party.

This was during the Cold War and it should not have surprised me. In the following years when anyone sounded paranoid about being spied upon, I was always inclined to believe them!

Chapter 5.

Formidable women

There is something else you need to know about my background. I had not been born into the Home Counties – I was an imposter. I still am an imposter.

I had been born on the edge of a Lancastrian mill town, just after the war, in 1950. Mum and Dad were Londoners but had moved to Lancashire after the war for Dad's work and had moved back to South Eastern England when I was seven or eight. There, I had looked around middle class suburbia and seen things that I might not have noticed had I not been primed by a childhood in the glorious, egalitarian North.

I noticed when my teacher, Mr Evans, lashed out angrily at the little boys in our class but sat the pretty little girls on his knee to explain their sums. While the boys walked down our road towards the council estate, their heads bowed into the wind or rain, Mr Evans would drop me off at my door in his little red car and wave cheerily to my attractive mother. Even at nine years old, though I liked Mr Evans, I recognised that this was not right.

I also recognised that the school's streaming system was based on some secret, insidious method which had something to do with the way you spoke – I had a Darwen accent then and accents are catching. I was placed in the 'B' stream. I knew, though Mum would never admit it, that my reading was slow and stuttering and that I couldn't spell – I could accept my second-class status on those grounds, though did not know how on earth I was expected to do dictation when the teacher spoke with a north-south vowel shift making all the words different. What I couldn't understand was why that meant that I couldn't learn to sail – a privilege reserved for those who spoke the Queen's English and could read fluently and were in the 'A' stream. My mother understood all these things and sent me to Elocution – another hoop.

She also got wind of IQ tests which were soon to be incorporated into the 11-plus exam. She got a book of them from the library – they were fun – we worked through the whole book and I got quite good at them!

My mother did many things.

I was not good at getting up in the mornings; Mum would waltz into my room at 7:30 am and fling back the curtains with an up-beat weather forecast, I would groan and shrink beneath my covers.

My mother would return chattering optimistically and open the window wide, admitting the frosty air – no centrally heated warm air to conserve in those days. I would emit a muffled sob.

She would return again, 'Coffeeee!'

'I'm awake… Go away!'

'No, you're not!' and off came the covers, ripped off by the matriarch with the flourish of a bull-fighter.

My mother never understood just how bad I felt in the mornings but, had my father not felt just as bad himself, as he was being dressed by his wife, he might have acknowledged his daughter's difficulties. As it was, he was far too angry. Dad and I stomped and growled at each other on the narrow landing of our semi-detached home as the irrepressible wife and mother became even more cheery and animated, secure in the knowledge that she was indispensable to the essential daily mobilisation of her family. Getting us up was her job and, God knows, she felt that there was little enough of importance in her life for the rest of the day.

It is not surprising therefore that on occasions I missed the bus. On one such occasion I returned home to increase my mother's self-worth by commissioning her to ferry me to school by car only to find that she had already left on another mission. So it was that I cycled the 5 miles or so to school. I arrived much earlier than I had feared and felt quite bushy-tailed and alert.

Thenceforth I had an extra fifteen minutes in bed and biked to school and by the time I got to the end of the road I felt almost human. On the strength of this, Dad also bought a bike and rode it once.

As I sped out of town with my head down, leaning into the bends, a small, pale-blue Morris 1100 would often over-take me tooting cheerfully. It was Miss Hasslingdon. As we hit the morning traffic by the turning for the station in the old town, I could sometimes catch her up and pass the stationary headmistress with a ding of my bell. Then I would pedal like fury to get up the hill and into school without hearing a second triumphant toot.

If it was frosty or misty or there was snow on the ground I would still go for the bus, but now I didn't have to wait so long because Miss Hasslingdon, if she saw me waiting, would pick me up and we would chat all the way to school.

Miss Hasslingdon was considered by her students to be an anachronism, an antique – middle-aged and narrow minded – fat and frumpy. She certainly made no concessions to fashion, did not dye her wiry, salt and pepper coloured hair which was probably cut in exactly the same way as it always had been, since before her mother died – Miss H lived with her widowed father whom she must have brought with her from Lancashire. She wore no make-up and always had sensible shoes – no slip-offs, as she insisted on calling the new trendy slip-ons.

Under this carapace of eccentricity Miss H communicated a sense of importance to her pupils – their own importance and the importance of education and their own education in particular.

But… She had a fairly nippy car which she drove quite fast and under close interrogation she admitted to visiting interesting places at the weekends. She went to the theatre, did long distance walks, talked a lot about her nieces and nephews, went on foreign holidays with friends and above all, she was interested in what other people did and thought. She talked about her garden and her cat and was intrigued by my stories from the vets where I had gone for work experience and been taken on to 'help out' twice a week after school and on Saturday mornings.

As each pupil tried to remain un-noticed by the Headmistress, make no mistake – the Headmistress had plans for them all.

She was mindful of how ill-prepared some of the girls were for the life that they might find after school – perhaps harping back to her own early days at Cambridge, she wanted to prepare them socially for what might await them. She had a little money at her disposal, in the Governors' Fund, which she used to employ Mrs Cholmondley-Sheringham, an under-employed Oxford arts graduate. This plummy lady would prepare girls for the Oxford and Cambridge entrance examinations. A small group was selected for twice weekly tutorials to discuss extracurricular subjects: current affairs, politics, philosophy and the arts. Once every three month or so the group would convene at Mrs Cholmondley-Sheringham's beautiful home where it was hoped that girls would learn the art of small talk, how to pronounce certain tricky names (Dalziel, Cockburn etc) and what to do with fish knives and how not to put milk in Earl Grey tea. Coffees were discussed and tasted, napkins folded, the filling of ramekins and basic oenology was covered (not forgetting that on a limited budget, inviting guests for afternoon tea was quite acceptable) – but all too late for poor Miss Hasslingdon.

She had studied Chemistry at Cambridge, which was not so very far away, and when we entered the sixth form, she took a handful of likely candidates to visit her alma mater. This included coffee with some of Miss H's old students (from her previous school) now studying at the Cambridge, ladies' college, New Hall.

We met in a prize winning ultra-modern hall of residence in the study suite of one of these glamorous long haired, long legged university students. There was a mezzanine with staggered stairs – different steps for left and right feet, we had great fun practicing running up and down and watching the leather mini-skirted students show how it was done, making strange shadows in the pools of contemporary light. It was odd to see how fond these sophisticated young women seemed of Miss H – how relaxed they were with her.

She took us for lunch at the hot and heaving Copper Kettle Café, paid for from the Governors Fund. I had steaming shepherd's pie with carrots and peas.

Then a handsome young man gave us a guided tour of Trinity College, gave my friend, Pat, his phone number and regaled us with tales of under-graduate high jinks – of Morris Minors deconstructed by engineering students and re-constructed on the roof of the mighty Chapel. He touched his finger against his lips to hush us and took us into the academic heart of the place, the great Library, a three-dimensional polished wood and leather-bound labyrinth, amber lighted and silent, where students sat with heads bent over books undisturbed, it seemed, for hundreds of years.

Last of all we sat opposite the choir in the famous King's College Chapel to listen to sung evensong. I looked up at the great stone fans that rose above them in the vaulted ceiling as little boys' angel voices rose above the older choristers and I imagined them flitting on white wings in and out of the stone arches.

*

By then I was very focused on studying medicine and mindful of the length of the course and the cost to my parents so was reluctant to wait another year to try seriously for Oxbridge. I had studied the statistics and worked out the relative chances of acceptance by the various colleges, corrected for gender and back-ground. My best chance would seem to be a college in England (not Scotland or Wales) and one that had been until recently a women's college – to lead by example the only women's college in Britain had, ironically, just reduced the number of women admitted to 50% in the hope that the other colleges would increase the proportion that they took from the present miserable 8-10%.

One great advantage of choosing the Royal and Ancient Hospital School of Medicine for Women was that it was a twenty-minute train ride and a short walk from home. There was to be another advantage.

When I stood in front of Dame Cecily Bagshott at my Royal and Ancient interview I felt oddly at ease. The spiky grey hair, the broken veins on the Dean's shiny nose, the worn tweed suit (with the faintest whiff of tobacco) and the brown, Clark's sandals all seemed familiar – to represent someone who would put her students first – who was on my side. Above all, the hint of amused irony (designed to be un-nerving to the unprepared) was reassuring – inviting.

'Now, Miss Grant, what is it that makes you think that our humble and under-funded institution can fulfil your complex educational needs? We note that we are your first choice, above New Hall and Newnham Colleges, Cambridge, both venerable and wealthy institutions.'

I told her exactly why I preferred to study at a college that, though poor, had impeccable credentials for the education of women and where there would be absolutely no risk of me having to complete my studies at a male dominated teaching hospital where I might be treated as a second-class student or an amusing novelty – here I was confident that I would be judged on my ability and nothing else.

'My Goodness, are you a dangerous feminist?' asked the old gentleman with white whiskers who sat to the right of the Dean,

27

representing the University of London.

Not at all! I reassured him that he had no cause to feel threatened as how could I feel disadvantaged by my gender in an environment where all my role models would be women?

'Well, almost all, Sir!' I added with my mother's dazzling smile.

The following October, you guessed, I was queuing on the huge rectangular, oak staircase that was at the heart of the Royal and Ancient – it was never polished, on principle. We were waiting for our locker keys while a formidable lady in a tweed suit from the Registry (the seat of all power) explained how much worse it could have been if, as mooted, the ladies had had to share their facilities with all the troublesome new gentlemen. 'Fortunately, we decided to give the men a temporary erection in the quadrangle!'

But first – there was the long summer vac.

Chapter 6.

Real Life

The fortnight after leaving school had been a time of transition, when novels are supposed to be set and may still be, one day.

Jane and I had gone to France on our own for a camping holiday, had met Frenchmen and tasted strange and delicious things. Jane had fought off the unwanted attentions of one of these aforementioned with nothing but a baguette, well more of a military-weight *pain rustique,* and I had received an equally unwanted offer of marriage from another.

It seemed that more had happened in the fortnight since leaving school than had occurred in the previous several years but now it was time to buckle down and earn some money.

Lesson one: it's not what you know but who you know!

Both my parents now worked at the headquarters of the large, international chemical company that was situated in our town. They travelled by car but so large was the workforce and so unimaginative were the working hours that it took as long to get into and off the site in a car as it would have taken to commute to London.

I had finally passed my driving test in the previous December, having at last completed it (on the third attempt) without mounting the kerb or going the wrong way up a one-way-street. I still needed practice (preferably supervised or at least 50% supervised). Thus, for the last six months I had been taking my parents, and two of their colleagues who lived around the corner, to work – dropping them at a small pedestrian entrance in the security fence near to their offices and collecting them at precisely 17:02 hrs. Although emotionally traumatic, being driven by his daughter, it gave my father great satisfaction to retrieve sixty minutes each day from the company to which he had sold his soul after the war and it got them all home to the sherry bottle half an hour earlier.

Eileen was the lady passenger and probably the one who conceived this wheeze – an early reversed variant of the school run (which never caught on). She was a clever, hard-nosed businesswoman, known on the site as the *Queen of the Fairies* being Manager of Office Services, a job no man would take on – in charge of the 2000 women employed in secretarial and clerical positions and subject to all the woes and secret maladies of their gender which were still a mystery to any male middle manager in 1968.

On the Monday after my 18th birthday Eileen arranged for me to start work as a temporary junior clerical officer at a salary of £8 per week, paid monthly. This left my week-ends free for early morning shifts at a petrol station on the A1 and my week-day nights for bar work.

'Never go round the offices after 2pm on a Friday,' warned Eileen.

'Okey-dokey,' said I without even asking the reason why, so many other work-related injunctions were rolling around in my head.

By the second Friday I had just about mastered the job –I had worked out the lay out of the place, discovered all the out-lying and tucked-away labs, storerooms and security kiosks that occasionally got mail. I had the whole place mapped out in my head and sorted the mail to deliver seamlessly and without doubling back. My morning work was done by 11am and I could get the afternoon round done by 2pm. The main problem was boredom, but I made myself useful; photocopying, filing, making cups of tea and washing up. So, on Friday afternoon when there was a late delivery of a small parcel for someone in the accounts department, I looked at my watch and saw that there were still two interminable hours to go – I chirped up, 'I'll pop that over to Accounts, it's right the other side – it'll give me something to do!'

As I entered the large open-plan office I sensed immediately that something was different – instead of the normal throng of activity with young men sitting upright at desks clicking away at adding machines, half the workstations were empty. Those that were there seemed befuddled and dishevelled. It was hot but they were not just in their shirt sleeves but had shed their ties and they sprawled lugubriously, seeping perspiration. As I walked briskly past, their eyes followed me. I was aware of the humid, musk laden atmosphere as several pairs of blood-shot eyes seemed to creak as they were cranked round to follow me. I made haste to the manager's office and knocked.

'Come!'

Someone behind me sniggered as I opened the manager's office door and walked in brandishing the little parcel. A red faced, fat man, who looked old, was almost horizontal in his chair, he had had his back to me as I entered, the reason for which I could not see. He spun round on the swivel and looked me deliberately up and down, 'Well Hallo my little darling – I haven't seen you before.'

'I've been doing the mail for a couple of weeks, Sir – there's a parcel for you –I should think it's a book.' He was rising from his chair and was bearing down on me surprisingly nimbly. He was behind me and he was closing the door. His other hand was already resting on my shoulder.

Lesson 2:
Never let a potential assailant come between you and the door
(2a: always park for escape).

I knew a bit about animals, I had worked at the vets – I didn't try to pull away but walked around his desk to the far side, looking interested in his lair. As he followed me his hand slid down my arm to my elbow and thence to my waist where it was creeping round to the front and down towards my groin. I skipped around his important looking chair, turned, unwrapping his arm and thrust the parcel at him which he took automatically with both hands, then I darted to the door and fled, slamming it behind me. I could hear him laughing.

'They are all half-cut on Friday afternoons,' I told my father, 'They can't do any work – that's a 10% reduction in productivity – isn't that your job Dad – productivity!'

'Chalk it up to experience , dear! Eileen did try to warn you.'

'It's a bloody jungle!'

That was probably the truth of the matter and it was a lesson well learned but there was much more...

In the evenings I worked at a little pub near the back door of the company, where we all now worked and where there was a large garage in which the directors' chauffeur driven cars were kept and maintained, polished, and valeted and kept roadworthy. I sometimes took them mail when I would nod to the waiting drivers. I was on good terms with them and was gratified when I started work at the pub to find the same group of men having their lunch in the public bar – a liquid lunch. It was not unusual for these immaculate, uniformed chauffeurs to down 4 pints of Guinness in a lunch break and 6 to 8 pints before setting off to drive a director to Heathrow in the evening.

This interested me, I had never before given much thought to the proclivities of the working man. The drink driving legislation had been introduced the previous year and the legal limit for blood alcohol to drive a car was 80 mg/100ml – a level achieved, I thought, by about a pint and a half of Guinness (maybe 2 pints in a chap with a big beer belly!) Breathalysers were already starting to be used by the police.

I asked my father how they could drink so much and still be professional drivers and whether that was the norm. He wondered if they were so experienced and driving so much second nature to them, that alcohol didn't make much difference. He thought it *was* perhaps the norm. At any rate he was not surprised.

I was shocked; new wave morality was starting – sex before marriage was starting to be okay but those of us on the moral high ground were looking suspiciously at those around us to reinforce our position in other ways, with other things on which to focus our God-given quantity of outrage! Eventually one would be free to end one's sentence with a preposition, but woe betide the woman who would buy her child a *full-fat* yoghurt or fail to care about her plastic waste. This leaves those at the top end of the age range perpetually bemused by the new taboos! When one has spent ones younger days fighting off sexual assaults and attempted rape it is difficult to get excited about an inappropriate pronoun.

Lesson 3: don't assume everyone else is just like you.

(Failure to heed this maxim would lead to the political chaos of the 2010s.) Oh, and don't drink and drive. It would be several years before I could even afford to, and 29 years before the whole nation would understand the reality of a professional driver so experienced and driving so automatically that alcohol hadn't seemed to make much difference![2]

On Saturday morning at 6 o'clock Mum got me up and drove me to the garage on the A1 – perhaps a 10-mile round trip, repeated at 2pm

2. *The death of Princess Diana, August 1997*

(unless they wanted to do the weekly shop without a car). It was my first shift at the fuel station.

'For Christ sake, if you are in any doubt about what fuel to use or where to put it, ask the driver! And the same goes for any ladies wanting you to top up their oil or their screen wash!' said Dad, who had struggled onto the landing with superhuman willpower to bestow this counsel of bitter experience before collapsing back into bed.

I was to sit in a little kiosk on the forecourt, quite chilly at that time in the morning. There was just enough to do to prevent me doing anything like studying but not enough to stop me being bored. It wasn't quite as bad as working in a factory which I had done once before when my father had made me continue for a whole week of mind-numbing repetitive labour – I had wilfully insisted on taking the work despite his advice. The eight-hour petrol station shift was interminable, punctuated only by lorry drivers wanting to sell me stolen property.

'That's really kind of you but I don't know what I'd do with a pack of five lavatory seats.'

'You could sell 'em Darling, that's what you do!'

'Gosh, I don't think I'd be allowed to do that… But thank you all the same.' Another lorry driver climbed back into his cab shaking his head.

I had unwittingly discovered the 5% rule – that (at least in times of full employment) hauliers were entitled to 5% of any cargo – this was called 'wastage' or 'falling off the back of the lorry'. 'Bunse' [3] my father explained (turning over a paper clip in his hand while resting the other on the company desk diary in which he did the family's accounts) was pretty well institutionalised. There were unwritten rules about it and, provided no one took advantage, everybody turned a blind eye. It introduced a profit motive into an otherwise boring and low paid job. It could even improve productivity and retention of employees who might otherwise be tempted by more interesting or better paid work – you see there is much more satisfaction in a little fiddle than from any amount of honest toil! It seemed that had I purchased the 5 lavatory seats at much less than cost price and then sold them on during the

3. *Bunse : Cockney rhyming slang: Bunsen burner: nice little earner.*

week to other motorists at a profit my boring job would have been much more satisfying.

Lesson 4.
Economics and sociology are more complicated than they seem.

Someone else must have been thinking along these lines because soon after, so that employees at head-office, without access to manufactured goods, could benefit more from what they invested in their work, the company opened a works shop with large discounts on the company's products and those of its subsidiaries —paints, thinners, de-icer, tar to mend the hole in your roof, cellular blankets, plastic lavatory seats (!) etc – the paper clip had come of age! My mother went to work there.

By the end of summer, I had worked out that, were I not going into medicine, I would much rather work in a pub than in a factory, a shop (I'd done that before), an office or a petrol station where I felt people deserved every penny they earned. In the future to be paid generously for doing something that you love would never sit easily with me – it never seemed quite right.

Chapter 7.

Surface Anatomy.

When girls and boys, some straight from single sex schools, arrive at medical school they have an expectation – all the secrets of the human condition will soon be revealed to them. Nobody knew how they would cope with cutting up a dead body (dissection was a major part of the pre-clinical course in 1968). Simply entering the anatomy room for the first time was a big deal. I had helped the vet with post-mortems but the nearest I had come to a dead human was a large dead pig.

When the vet opened the abdomen there had exploded a great cloud of foetid gas and (it suddenly dawned upon the vet) spores which under cursory examination, with the microscope, looked a bit like anthrax! (I told you everyone could do everything in those days.) I had been sent home with a note for my doctor to give me large doses of penicillin and told to keep myself in quarantine until further notice! Miss Hasslingdon had volunteered that my sick note on that occasion was considered an all-time-great and had been pinned up in the staff room.

I turned my head just a little as I passed the open door of the Long Room, the anatomy lab. where the rows of shrouded corpses lay patiently on galvanised trollies, waiting for their new young doctors. The vet had maintained that most nasty bugs were species specific (except anthrax) which prompted me to wonder what had killed off these members of my own species.

There were other anxieties for us young people, there was blushing and fainting and throwing up or, worst of all, being found out for sexual ignorance, like the poor young man (not even so very young – but he *was* a Christian). He was filling out a fertility questionnaire with a pretty, married but childless young woman patient, within earshot of other students.

'How many times a week do you engage in sexual intercourse?'

'About, let me see...eight times perhaps.'

'But how can that be? There are only seven nights in a week!' The laughter followed him for years, probably still does as the tale is told and re-told with gales of hilarity even from those, like himself, who are still not quite sure why it is so funny.

The venerable ladies of the Royal and Ancient had a plan for all these, flushing, sweating, palpitating and fainting young people. It was called Surface Anatomy.

It was thrust upon us without warning on the first day. We had all received instructions to attend for the first week with swimming costumes and track suits. We had assumed this was for sport – not for easy access to each other's nearly naked bodies. The year's intake was split into groups of six, three young ladies, and three young gentlemen. To each group a senior student was allocated: a demonstrator, and all had clip boards and work sheets and off we went to explore the outside of the human body – our own human bodies. That is all except the Chief Rabbi's daughter who went to the Registry for further negotiation.

The programme was exhaustive – every bony prominence was marked with felt pen, every palpable tendon insertion, pulse, ligament and funny-bone identified, named and noted. Young's modulus was applied to skin and the relative stretchiness of that organ in all its types and directions was tested and compared; scrotums and foreskins winning hand's down but disallowed due to suspected observer bias and the unwillingness of the subjects to allow independent verification. Genitalia and female breasts, you see, were the only parts kept covered, or not covered by the week-long course although the more conscientious and enthusiastic students may have made their own arrangements to rectify this deficiency. Lines were drawn down long bones and videos were made of locomotion, students waltzed with articulated skeletons and rummaged in each other's abdomens for spleens and livers. We hammered each other for reflexes, shoved each other, led each other around blindfold and shone lights into each other's orifices.

Graffitied young people in skimpy trunks and bikinis were encountered nipping out to the canteen for a coffee or shivering on the fire-escape having a smoke. Clinical students popped back to the pre-clinical school to have a look at the new year's intake and discarded inhibitions lay scattered on the floor with the crumpled track suits. The scruffy, friendly old building was alive with animated young people.

The idea seemed to be to heap so much embarrassment onto the students in the first couple of days that nothing else would ever bother us – it was flooding – a crude but effective psychological ploy. At that time Student Health was in the charge of an elderly lady psychiatrist of a Freudian bent – she insisted on doing cervical smears on lady students and teaching testicular self-examination to the male students while cross examining them about their mental health – that really wasn't cricket. However, nobody ever complained and if Surface Anatomy was her idea it certainly was a good icebreaker.

Many of the surface anatomy exercises took place in the Long Room, in between the parked trolleys of shrouded, dead bodies in an atmosphere of formaldehyde and embalming fluid. This gave time and opportunity for all the students, in their own time, to lift the corner of a shroud and meet their new colleague – each group of six students had their very own body for the semester. Mrs Enid Evans, age 78 of Wandsworth (Myocardial infarction) was pleased to meet me.

During the first term I commuted from home, biking to the station and taking the early train and returning at bedtime. This had seemed quite doable in anticipation – I would crawl out of bed, dress in the dark, grab a banana and leave without any fuss before the family awoke.

The practice was very different – my mother insisted on the established routine – she would get up first, dress and be in her right-mind to manage and chivvy my departure – to turn all my awakening pain and associated resentment and anger upon her – to sacrifice herself to the process, to insist that I sat and ate my cooked breakfast and to make sure I looked tidy. She also insisted on staying up to see me safely home, debriefed and fed, which wasn't necessary as I had eaten in college with my friends before spending my evening in the Long Room or the Library.

As I tried to live two lives, the situation just wasn't viable: 'Mum, if you don't just let me slip in and out un-noticed you are going to wear yourself to a frazzle. I'm the one that's at university, I have to make the effort – not you. The other students have digs all over the place, but they just go back to sleep and that's what I want to do. We can have a chat and eat together at the week-ends.'

'Huh! You'll never get up in the morning!'

That was my mother's last word on the subject; just before Christmas and after discussing the matter with Dad, I managed to get a place for the following term at a hall of residence in Bloomsbury.

Chapter 8.

The way my mum saw it.

'*It is 1968 and I am forty-five years old, middle-aged by anyone's standard, but I can still turn a head and catch an eye with my quick smile. Didie has my smile and my eyes, but I suppose she gets her brains from her father – his family have all been clever although the women weren't any use to man nor beast. (My mother worked until she was eighty-four and even now, at ninety, she keeps house for my bachelor brother, Peter, although I help her a bit.)*

I've been married for twenty-five years – hard to believe it – I was a child bride! (That's what I tell people). I was actually twenty and a virgin and we were married on the weekend before D-Day (the first day of the Normandy Landings in the Second World War, Geoff went up Omaha Beach on D-day plus1). If the wind had been in a different direction Geoff's leave could have been cancelled and we'd never have been married. I know that because he was a different person when he came back from the war. If we hadn't married in '44 we certainly wouldn't in '47. There had been too much water under the bridge. He never talked about it but he saw things … My brother, Peter was the same – he's never married. Didie says that when they get together that's all old-people talk about: the war. I suppose it's true, but they don't tell you the bad things – the things that wake them screaming in the night. When Geoff came home, he and I were like strangers.

I worked throughout the blitz, in Holborn, I taught telephonists (the buildings either side of ours were bombed out); Didie says that must have been when I became such a snob about accents, where I started judging people by how they sound – her dad is very well spoken, not that he says much these days. We all had to do our bit and I helped after work in a WVS[4] canteen for the ARP[5], the fire watchers and the firemen – we had a laugh. I used to come home on the tube from Holborn to Highgate, past all those poor people sleeping on the platforms – I hated that, there

---

4. *Women's Voluntary Service*
5. *Air Raid Precautions*

were loud, vulgar women and they'd swear at me if I stepped over the line that marked their area. I couldn't have slept there. Quite often the train stopped at Archway and I'd walk from there, my dad would come and meet me and sometimes we'd stand on the Archway Bridge and watch the fires burning in the City.

I stopped work as soon as Geoff was demobbed (respectable, married women didn't work then) and Peter got Geoff a job in Industry, up North, with his company. I was at home all day, knew no-one, had a tiny damp little cottage to look after and everyone so uncouth and over friendly – you couldn't keep them out of your kitchen.

Geoff should really have gone to university, he had a place at Manchester, but I was pregnant, and the place wasn't for a couple of years – we had to get on with our lives. I had terrible back ache and when the baby was due, I went down to London to stay with my family and I went to the private wing of the Royal Northern Hospital for the delivery. The little boy was born dead. The cord had come down first and the trainee doctor couldn't do anything – I remember, he was distraught – I felt sorry for him, I think he was more upset than I was.

If I'd been at home in the North, I'd have been at the Royal Infirmary with the mill-girls and the factory workers, where they did thousands of deliveries and I'd have been whistled along for a Caesarean section and I'd have a son of nearly twenty... But then I wouldn't have Didie – they, the doctors, told me to get pregnant again immediately and that is what we did – I was very focused on the second baby that I was carrying, very fearful for it, very tired and run-down, I had terrible backache again in the second pregnancy and was very unhappy. I've never told anyone before but that was the time that Geoff had an affair, with 'his little Edna'. That is something I don't talk about.

I was frightened – more frightened than I ever was in the Blitz. I had never felt so alone. I got the train and went back to London, but Daddy sent me straight back – to my husband and my duty. Daddy died before the baby was born.

Edna emigrated to Australia.

This time the baby was born in Lancashire, Diana was the most beautiful thing I had ever seen, but she wouldn't feed from me. She was jaundiced, and every time the midwife weighed her she had lost more *weight and it was all my fault. In the end, after three miserable months, they put her on the bottle and she never looked back.*

Geoff had nightmares for years, I couldn't leave him alone with Diana. He was so jumpy, if you made him jump, he would lash out. He was so irritable. When Diana was little, I made sure she was in bed by the time he got home but when she was older we'd all have lunch together at the week-end and if she upset him (it was usually her table manners) he used to slap her round the head but he wasn't a bad man – I always thought it was the war. He never got drunk and he never hit me on purpose.

Things are different these days, women can work and don't have to be dependent on a man. Diana will be able to support herself, if she needs to, but I couldn't. I couldn't have left Geoff, even if I had wanted to and, anyway, what I wanted had nothing to do with anything. Marriage meant something then, and I certainly wasn't the sort of woman who would slip from one marriage to another by having an affair or by stealing someone else's husband. Anyway, I had Diana.'

Chapter 9.

The Long Room – the aberrant pancreas

The anatomy laboratory in the long attic of the medical school was where most relationships were forged and where pre-clinical medical students acquired their characteristic aroma. There were six students to each body. The system was that one student held the book and read out what should be seen, what nerves and arteries were about to be revealed or destroyed without being noticed, while a second wielded the scalpel. A third would be nursing a hang-over, seated on a tall stool, resting his head on his folded arms on another part of the otherwise shrouded corpse – no one thought this disrespectful. The fourth would be entertaining the operators, the scalpel driver and the navigator, with his or her witty repartee – this one was destined to be an anaesthetist whose prime function would always be to entertain his colleagues during repetitive procedures, more to do with keeping the surgeon awake than the patient asleep. A fifth would be browsing the other bodies and the museum, where a pre-prepared specimen showed what should be found – and chatting. This student was intelligence gathering and would return periodically to the work in progress to advise and pass comments on other students' breasts, legs, eyes, smiles, the charm of the demonstrator and, occasionally, someone's discovery of an aberrant subclavian artery or an absent gall bladder. The sixth student was invariably absent – learning it all from books at home, or not.

Apart from the anaesthetist, the roles rotated as we dug our way, layer by layer through Enid Evans of Wandsworth who quite enjoyed the company of the young people.

The Long Room with its rows of bodies, Victorian orangery skylights, free-wheeling angle-poise lamps on tripwires and grubby-short-white-coated students had different moods. Bright and studious by day, with visits from academic staff who would glide up and down in long, pristine, white coats. They would occasionally divert to peer into a body cavity at the request of a pushy or a genuinely flummoxed student. Then other students, mainly browsers, would gather round for hints and pearls of wisdom to carry back to their own team.

Sometimes these visits were uninvited and accompanied by merciless cross-examination. Students were challenged robustly in those days, put under pressure – students were not assumed to have feelings. 'Young man, if you could muster one more neurone you might manage a synapse!'

The anatomy laboratory was open six days a week from 8am to 11pm. After dark the Long Room was very different with its dome of dark sky above drifting down to fill all the corners. Pools of electric light from one or two angle-poise lamps bathing the occasional figure, hunched over a glowing body, while the shadows played around the intervening rows of draped cadavers.

I loved the Long Room at night; I wished I wore a long serge skirt and button boots under my white coat and had horn-rimmed, Victorian spectacles through which to peer into my dissection. I felt like a pioneer, like Mary Wesley canoeing up the Gambia River. In fact, I probably felt like Florence Rhind Grant (Granny Grant's Great Aunt) whose name, completely unknown to me at the time, was emblazoned on a plaque, half-way up the great scruffy staircase that led to the Long Room. She had dissected by oil lamp at the same table in 1883, she got the Gold Medal that year, and was the real pioneer.

In this unchanging, under-funded institution, eighty-five years later, in 1968, one or two other students were in the Long Room that night, catching up on their dissection, book propped on an arm, held by the helpful subject. These were often the students that wasted the most time chatting during the day or the ones with the dingiest digs – like Gary, the chap from Bradford, a Rugger playing, beer drinking, hoot by day but a secret surgeon by night. He would loom out of the darkness, allowing his face and unruly hair to shine in the light, and, that night, point out where the bile duct was taking a short-cut through the unusually annular head of Enid's pancreas.

'Gosh! Is that abnormal?' I asked.

'I think it's just a natural variant – you'd better find out before old Tweed swoops down on it. Dr Tweed was the Senior Lecturer, a middle-aged man with black hair, slicked down by Brylcreem and repression, who had spent his working life under the jackboot (or

Clark's sandal) of the two lady (formidable) anatomy professors – or so the students supposed. His only joy was in demonstrating, publicly, the ignorance of students and embalming anyone else who did not move – or so the students supposed.

Now I took off my gloves and adjourned to the museum, which was just a few work benches by the door where there were placed relevant elegantly dissected examples of what we were supposed to be seeing that week, some pretty resin casts of the blood supply and anatomy tomes with bookmarks in the appropriate sections. Tonight, there was also an open and half consumed packet of crisps and a few crumbs.

'Help yourself,' said Ruth from the shadows, 'I saw a rat here last night, but I didn't have anything to offer it... I like rats.' So started a lifelong friendship.

'Do you know how common an annular pancreas is?'

'... No.'

Silence ensued. Ruth was not like other girls, certainly not like most of the girls at medical school – confident in their above average intelligence and good looks – or so I supposed.

'Here we are – annular pancreas – *autopsy prevalence 10 per 100,000,* that's 1 in 10,000 – I can remember that.'

'This book says 1 in 250 dissections,' interjected Ruth helpfully.

'Thanks – nothing is ever simple!'

'Shhh.' Ruth froze but indicated with the slightest flick of her eye that there was something in the shadow at the end of the bench. We both kept completely still. A large brown rat came out of the shadow and approached the crumbs, he walked past them with only a cursory twitch of his whiskers and proceeded to the packet, lying open on the bench. He nosed it open taking a large crisp and then withdrew to the shadow to crunch it. The clock struck eleven and we collected our things – you wouldn't want to be locked in all night. Ruth picked up the packet of crisps but left the crumbs. 'He'll eat those by morning.' It was forbidden to bring food into the Long Room.

'You are not going to finish that packet, are you?'

'No, I'll keep it for him for tomorrow night.'

*

The following afternoon Dr Tweed did swoop.

'Ah... And what have we here?' He pointed at an ill-defined and rather ragged mound of pale tissue with a pointer that he kept clipped in the top packet of his lab coat, but didn't actually touch it...

'Is it an annular pancreas, sir?' asked the navigator who had been briefed.

'You know, I do believe it is... Very good. Tell me more.'

He who was hung over stretched himself to his full height, paled even more and nearly fell off his stool. The other four looked at each other then three of them looked at me.

'It's an uncommon variant, Sir,' I said.

'Indeed... How uncommon?'

'Well sir, I think that depends on who is looking for it.' He looked surprised, shocked – his eyes bore into me. 'I mean if it's a pathologist at an autopsy, he'll find about one in every 10,000 autopsies. But if it's a proper anatomist who's dissecting the subject the rate rises to about one in 250.'

'Very good, Miss Grant,' said the proper anatomist. 'Exactly so! So what do you suppose is the likelihood of such an uncommon variant being picked up by medical students?'

'Not high, Sir.'

'Unless of course they are budding anatomists. Eh? Miss Grant.'

Thus, I progressed through the anatomy hoop – absorbing knowledge which often perfused me quite passively, like the smell of the Long Room.

The following evening the crisps were again open on the museum bench and Ruth was bent over her anatomy book. Her long black hair (tied back during the day) was loosed and fell over her shoulders. She had thick jam-jar-bottom glasses with heavy black frames and, from where I was, I could only see Ruth's pale nose protruding from its black carapace – very close to the book. Actually, rather like her friend, the rat, peeping out of a shadow.

'I didn't notice you wore glasses yesterday,' I observed.

'Contacts! My eyes are sore today, I think it's the formalin... Don't be offended if I ever cut you dead ... I'm almost blind – I didn't realise trees had leaves until I was ten!' She had a slow way of talking, quite relaxing after a day of the feverish enthusiasm and competitiveness of the other freshers. But every phrase left you in doubt as to whether she had finished or was looking about in her head for the next word she needed.

Ruth took me to see her body's bi-cornuate uterus – another variant.

'Like a sheep!' I said.

'Not really... Only the name... Sheep wombs actually are like two horns... This is just a bit misshapen with a partial septum.'

'When did you last look inside a sheep?'

'My big sister's married to a sheep farmer in Yorkshire (they lamb about a thousand ewes) ... And my next sister (she's the clever one), she's a vet in Leeds... The last couple of years, when I was at crammer, I went up at Easter to help.'

'I can't imagine what it must be like to have sisters – I'm an only one. There's a lot of pressure being an only one.'

'I'm the fourth of five... Dad wanted a boy – I think they almost gave up in disgust when they produced me – a fourth girl... I think I was always destined to be a disappointment... And then along came my little brother... I love him but I worry about him... He smokes too much dope... He'll be lucky if he doesn't get rusticated from Cambridge.'

'Wow! You're a high achieving family.'

'I guess *they* are – I'm the black sheep, it took me five years to get the grades to get in here, poor Dad, I've cost him a fortune... He's very neurotic... I had three interviews (Mum's an old student).' Ruth slid her spectacles down her nose to look over the top and impersonate the Dean, '*Ah... Miss Benedict. Back again. Struggled up a few more grades, have we? Yes, I see, a 'C' in Chemistry – shame about the Physics – perhaps we'll see you again next year...*'

'Still, they kept on seeing you. That must have been encouraging?'

'Mum has always worked full-time as a GP in the Leeds inner city, even when we were tiny... That was the key... You know, they are still frightened about wasting all this education on us...'

'Cooee! Anybody there?' Someone was waving from just outside the door of the Long Room.

'Christ! It's Bette!' I ran the length of the dark laboratory. Bette was an eccentric school friend, 'What are you doing here?'

'Visiting you. The nice porter said I could come up.'

'You are a *stranger* – you can't come in here!'

'It's spooky' she said, coming in. 'Can I look at a body – I'm a writer, I need atmosphere. Are they real?' She indicated the rows of parked trollies with the shrouded cadavers.

'Oh God!' I breathed.

'Give her a white coat then no one will notice her if they do come in.' said a young man's voice. 'Someone's left one by the door.'

'This smells of death – how delicious.'

'Bette!'

'Sorry! Oow, crisps, can I have one.'

'No, they are for the rat.'

'A white laboratory one, can I hold it?'

'No, a big brown sewer rat with a scaly tail,' said Ruth.

'Here! Catch!' shouted Gary tossing something like a rugby ball at Bette, amazingly she caught it.

'This is heavy, what is it?'

'A liver!'

'A model.'

'No, a real one – it's pickled.' To her credit, Bette placed the object carefully on the bench.

Perhaps this was the time when the differences started to be forged – the realism, the familiarity with death and the dead that has made me, for one, less sentimental, more rational about life and death than is now the norm. When I read today about the furore over the racehorse owner photographed sitting on a dead horse to take a phone call – the shock and the horror, I remember us lolloping on our draped old corpse as we leaned over to get a better view or just to rest an aching head – we meant no disrespect but we understood that it was a cadaver – not a person (a pickled liver not a pulsating, vital organ). Had I not been able to make this transition in my mind how could I ever have dissected Mrs Evans? Farmers, shepherds, racehorse breeders, soldiers, slaughter men, undertakers and doctors, we all have to deal with life and death – that doesn't make us psychopaths – we are just in a slightly different context from the rest of the world – less protected from its reality.

Chapter 10.

Hall

The first hall of residence that I tried was opposite the Union building where Ruth and I used to go occasionally for a swim in the basement pool – it was free and, as long as I didn't lose Ruth, we could be in and out and have a decent swim in under an hour. Once Ruth had removed her lenses, she was apt to attach herself to girls of a similar build and costume colour to mine and to wander off or to paddle through the foot bath into the gents' changing room. She didn't seem to pick up on things and I never could decide if this was due to her eyesight, attention or her hearing. Either way I found myself grabbing her arm at the edge of the pool or crossing the road. Getting around London must have been quite a challenge, even with contact lenses and a copy of the A to Z, no wonder Ruth occasionally found herself in strange places with strange people.

Ruth also wanted to get into a hall and double rooms were cheaper, so we went together and made enquiries at the austere reception desk where girls, more confident than ourselves were going in and out, picking up keys or tossing them to the porter with jolly quips. We were ushered in to see the President – a rather grand title for the ruling matriarch, a gentlewoman fallen upon hard times, who to our good fortune turned out to be quite snobby about subjects and very pro-medics and law students – they work so hard. There were no doubles available mid-semester, but they had one attic single and a shared double with room for one. I would have been wise to ask why the single bed in a double room had fallen suddenly and unexpectedly available – I did not.

The deal was done and after Christmas Ruth moved to the little attic garret and I moved to the floor below sharing with a lady theology student.

Ruth was no stranger to institutional life having attended an indecent number of different boarding schools and residential crammers. In those days the university authorities saw fit to protect the morals of their female students, they were after all *in loco parentis*, the age of majority was still 21 – the key of the door. Lady students (like chickens) were locked in at night and let out in the morning! They did not have the key to the door (except in extenuating circumstances – documented and signed for). Male friends could visit these fortified barracks provided they were signed in and out by the porter on the front desk, between 9am and 9pm. The authorities knew, like the ridiculed medical student in a previous chapter that sexual intercourse could only take place 7 nights a week – after 9pm!

Ruth took me to explore the lay out of the place – the nearest lavatory and, more important, the next nearest. The least used bathroom (in the attic where most of the rooms were used for storage) and the fire-exit (not in case of fire but to smuggle out late-night visitors or to send them out a different way in their own clothes in case of fire-drills which, for some reason, were frequent!)

In those days if you drove slowly down Malet Street at six o'clock on a Sunday morning it was not unusual to see a couple of hundred lady students in pyjamas aimlessly crowded on the pavement and spilling into the otherwise deserted road while elderly ladies in itchy brown dressing gowns, hair nets, a duty of care and clip boards tried to account for the milling throng.

If you slowed right down and looked carefully you might spot that one or two of the students were particularly hirsute. They had hairy, bare, muscular legs protruding from pink quilted dressing gowns and were shifting nervously from bare foot to bare foot and trying not to encounter the fire stewards taking the names and ticking them off their registers. It was a tribute to the ingenuity of these young lady-students and the power of a milling mob that although some of the names seemed to accrue more than one tick, everyone was always accounted for (even those who had signed-out for the weekend). There never ever was a real fire, thank God.

My new room-mate was Christened Penelope, that was how she first introduced herself and I did wonder, for that moment, whether it was hyphenated. She was studying Theology at King's although she never seemed to go there. She inhabited the room at all times, or so it seemed to me.

Ruth said: 'In my experience, girls who study Theology want to marry vicars... So why isn't she out there looking for one? You should ask her.'

At about 11pm I would let myself quietly into the room and, by the pink gloaming produced by the streetlamp shining through the tightly pulled red curtains, I would remove my clothes and slip into bed accompanied by loud sighing from the hump in the bed by the window.

In the morning, before her alarm went off, I would become aware of a muted voice (not very muted) praying for my immortal soul, asking God to save me, Diana – specifically by name, from sin!

'What does she think we do all day? Fornicate? Drink? Take drugs?'

'If only!' said Ruth longingly as we walked to college.

'She should see how hard we work, she told me they have one tutorial a fortnight and two lectures a week. We should take her in with us and show her our timetable.'

'Di, we spend most of our week cutting up old ladies... How do you think she'd view that...? Perhaps she knows already.'

'Oh... Maybe.'

'Puts fornication in its place!' We both laughed.

At the week-end Mum made a rich fruit cake for me to take back and share with Christened-Penelope.

'She probably just wants a friend not just someone who creeps in, in the dead of night, and slips out before dawn. That must be horrid.'

'Thanks Mum – I miss you!'

'I miss you too.'

Chapter 11.

Wheels on Fire

At about this time I was rather taken with a singer called Julie Driscoll. She sang *Wheels on Fire* on Top of the Pops with just the body language for what I wanted to say – but couldn't. She was slim with expressive arms that pointed and accused and wafted the smoke as she spun round to challenge the camera. I bleached my hair and had an elfin razor cut, piled on the mascara to make my eyes look like daisies and, at the weekends donned one of my skimpy culotte suits. Mum had made them with a Butterick pattern from two shimmering remnants that she found on St Albans market.

For a very short time in my life, I had the look that was me (well actually Julie Driscoll – but it fitted). I loved to dance and when I danced my body said what it wanted – it ignored its academic and professional stratagem and it forgot what my lifeguard had told me! It engaged young men on the dance floor in ways that did not properly advertise my vow of celibacy until after 2nd MB.

2nd MB was the exam that had to be passed by students before they progressed to clinical studies on live patients. It was judged that by that stage the university had invested enough effort in the student to allow for a more forgiving attitude to illness or pregnancy. Since the mishaps of my school days I had worked out that it would be difficult, almost dishonest, to advise obstetric and gynaecology patients or those in family planning and venereal clinics about sexual matters from a position of practical ignorance. So it was that I drew a metaphorical line in the sexual sand – that line was to be 2nd MB.

This I explained to Asher, another student at the Royal and Ancient, as we sat in his green MGB outside my hall of residence where he was dropping me off just before midnight (I had a key) after a hop at the medical school – 'Would you be interested in sharing a flat once we get on to clinical? Jim wants me to share, and a big, mixed flat would be good.'

'I don't know,' I said with mascara circled eyes. 'That's a long way ahead.' We kissed again – Asher was a very good kisser.

On the rare occasion that Christened-Penelope was absent, at home or on retreat, Asher, who lived at home in North London, was admitted (before 9pm) to my room. Then we would lie on my bed together and kiss, I hardly let him take off his over-coat. Not because of eagerness but because I wanted his dangerous potential wrapped as much as possible and he... Well, he didn't seem to know any better! He would lie, fully dressed, very still, balanced on my scissor closed body while our lips and tongues explored each other's sensuality while the rest of our bodies became hot and moist but remained chaste.

Sometimes at the weekends, Asher would drive me home and we would have a meal with my parents – Mum was impressed. Dad had misgivings.

One night we were on our way to a party and Asher wanted to pop into his home to pick up something.

'That'll be nice, I'd like to meet your mum and dad,' said I.

'Oh no! You can't do that, you'll have to wait in the car – Mum would go ape if I brought a non-Jewish girl home!'

I thought that was sad. Very sad. The more I thought about it, the more it troubled me.

'I don't see any future in a relationship that is completely unacceptable to one family.' I confided to Ruth.

'Yes, but you aren't planning on marrying him, are you?'

'No. But what is the point in starting any relationship that is doomed to failure, it seems like asking for heart-ache.'

'My trouble is I've always been rather keen on sex,' said Ruth. 'And I always persuade myself that every encounter has a... A future... By the way, you know Gary? Someone said he's got a girlfriend – a student at the LSE... Do you know if that is true?

'Oh, Ruth. You haven't? Have you?'

'Only the once... He's nice.'

'Yes, so's his girlfriend! She *is* at LSE – they're engaged.'

'Woops! That's a shame.' And Ruth looked sad.

The next time I was alone with Asher, I told him that I didn't want to get fond of him if he couldn't even tell his parents I existed – that was the end of it.

Jane was due to go up to Oxford in October but none of the rest of Miss Hasslingdon's hopeful Oxbridge candidates had been able to resist the offers of their various red-brick universities (a bird in the hand being infinitely preferable to any number in the bush). Perhaps that was for the best – none of them had been so inflexibly intellectual, political or just plain clever as to need an Oxbridge place. None except one – not Jane, she had a brother at Cambridge and had been persuaded by that sense of entitlement that pervaded his private school that there wasn't much point in applying for anywhere before you had your 'A' level results if you knew you were going to Oxbridge! Sibling rivalry may have also come into play.

The one girl who anyone could see needed to go to Oxford, and I don't doubt that Miss H did her best to persuade her, was Jennifer. Small, dark and unassuming, from a working class back-ground – she was the undisputed, cleverest person around (staff included). She was head and shoulders above the rest. She read Ovid and Virgil for pleasure (in the Latin) and taught herself Ancient Greek to read Aeschylus and Euripides. Her soft-spoken argument was that, to study archaeology, she needed to be near to the British museum, and she had a point.

She, like Bette, visited me at the Royal and Ancient. She also came after dark and walked the length of the Long Room, unperturbed by the ranks of the dead. She didn't want to peep under a shroud. She wanted to see the museum, not here – the main museum – 'You've got some of the best archaeological specimens of ancient human skulls in Britain!'

'Have we?' I exchanged surprised looks with the other students and then ushered Jennifer along the corridor towards the main Museum.

'Won't you have to get a key?' asked Jennifer.

'We'll see... Oh My God! It's Professor Benton-Lee, she's ancient but still does research... we shouldn't be...' A stooping figure with a stick, white hair, and a white coat nearly to the floor, was shuffling towards us and was now within earshot.

'Good evening Professor!' I managed to say. 'Will it be alright to take my friend into the museum – she's studying archaeology.

'Professor Benton-Lee? Professor Jessica Benton-Lee?' asked Jennifer (normally very quiet).

'The same!'

'I've just been reading your paper on the foramen spinosum in *Australopithecus.*'

'You had better come with me, My Dear, I'll show you the specimens and I've been dying to show someone our new *Paranthropus boisei,* it's only just arrived, on loan from New England.'

The professor took Jennifer by the arm and led her towards the museum.

'I'll leave you to it,' I said but nobody heard and, do you know (rhetorical), I never saw Jennifer again.

I heard that she had dropped out of university and this time I had an even stronger inkling that I knew the reason why – why would she want to surround herself with ignorant undergraduates?

I heard later that she was running her local Archaeology Society which was doing all sorts of research in exotic places and that she had a very well-paid job with the Inland Revenue, travelling to investigate complicated Trust fraud and off-shore scams particularly in the Middle East – that had a ring of truth – she wouldn't have any problem with Arabic, she had been teaching herself Aramaic in London. But every time I heard something new about Philby, Burgess, Maclean or Blunt the notorious Soviet spies of the 50s, I've found myself wondering about Jennifer (and what a marvellous cover an interest in archaeology would be). Had Jennifer been recruited by MI6 or perhaps the other side? What a clever way that would have been to finance her passion!

Chapter 12.

Guinness

The medical students' year was, and probably still is, regulated by the almanacs and 'anno-planners' produced by the various drug companies eager to seduce the doctors of the future before the hardening of their carapace of cynicism.

In the 1960s and 70s, with an eye to the potential profits in the management of chronic conditions (known as nice steady earners) companies invested heavily in forging relationships with students. The reps, who would become the brand managers and sales directors of the future pharmaceutical giants, were sent out, brimming with goodie bags, to woo the prescribers of the future. A student of the 1960s could be the bright young consultant of the 1980s, on the board of a Health Care Trust by the 1990s and an inaugural member of an advisory committee of the National Institute for Health and Care Excellence (NICE) by the end of that decade. This was called business strategy and was banned sometime in the eighties after an investigative journalist from a broadsheet caught a group of rheumatologists with their ethical pants down on the Orient Express.

This all started to become apparent to my parents after I telephoned one Friday evening to inform them that, contrary to the previous plan, I would not be home that evening as I had been invited to a 'drugs party'.

Mum sounded hesitant, she swallowed hard, 'That's nice dear! What sort of drugs would they be?' An excellent, if shaky, riposte from a woman confronting her worst nightmare.

There was a pause and muffled conversation at my end of the line, 'Ruth thinks it's a beta-blocker – I didn't know you were so interested in pharmacology? The reps are gathering us for a presentation in the Soho Hospital and then taking us out for a meal in China Town, they are taking over the whole restaurant – we can walk back to hall from there. It should be really good.'

'Righty-ho, Darling, have a lovely time!'

Appraising her husband of the situation, he saw it all. The novelty of a Chinese waiter, squeezing through the crowded tables offering crab: 'More crap meat', the students' suppressed giggles, the racism, the insipient corruption!

If you repeat a lie often enough, people will believe it:

'Guinness is good for you!'

'A Mars a day helps you work, rest and play!'

By 1968 the nation's liver was already causing concern as was the size of its belly. The physiology department of the medical school devised an experiment (probably at the instigation of that cunning Freudian student-health psychiatrist) to demonstrate the fallacy of both these statements to the students. The elegance of the plan was that we should find it all out for ourselves.

In the first week of the physiology semester, we were presented with measuring cylinders, scales, devices to test *reaction time* (medics are all very competitive), the kit for a complicated analytical procedure to determine blood alcohol levels, lots of syringes and needles and several litre bottles of vodka.

We were then invited to design experiments to prove that the group of students designating themselves as hardened drinkers could metabolise a given quantity of vodka more efficiently than the group who saw themselves as sober individuals. This could equally well have served, with slight modification to the analysis and statistics, as an experiment in a psychology module (had we had one!)

We compared the alcohol resistance of fat students to thin students and to heavy but muscular students. Then came the Mars bars – we were asked to deduce the relative effect on alcohol metabolism of Mars bars versus pure fructose (fruit sugar). Reaction times were scored throughout and the experiment was deemed to have reached an end point if the student fell from his or her tall, three-legged, lab stool or became unconscious.

Attendance was good, motivation for the tedious analytical process was excellent (everyone was keen to get their results), the deterioration in reaction times was unbelievable (and had to be repeated – may we have another bottle of vodka please!). One thin, boozy boy was so impressed by his appalling reaction times that he fitted a primitive, electronic, dexterity-tester into the ignition system of his mini-van – this was before drink driving had become an anathema and marked him out as a social pioneer – and much too clever for medicine.

Thus, conditioned with a comprehensive understanding of the effects of alcohol we students were ready for the next event in the scholastic year… The Guinness Walk.

First brewed in 1759 and still going strong after 200 years Guinness knew the power of brand loyalty and had its own business strategy. Guinness must be good for you – they'd had it in hospitals since before the inception of the National Health Service. Small bottles and later small cans, (one per patient per day) were given by this generous and altruistic company to every woman in hospital having, or just having had, a baby (a tacit acknowledgement of its contribution to conception in parts of the English-Speaking World).   It was also available to prescribe to other patients as a general tonic and pick-me-up. Because it was good for you!

Every year at the beginning of the summer term a healthy, sporting event was organised for all the medical students in London sponsored by the makers of the health-giving ale. For many years it had been a walk from London to Brighton along the A23, but the previous year there had been a fatality, so a safer route was planned from Box Hill to Brighton around the South Downs. The exact route is lost in the mists of memory – most of the competitors only remembering the first two stages – I recall a pleasant, convivial ramble on country paths and little-used lanes and over a stile to the first nine-mile check point. My friends and I had made quite good time considering that we had left towards the end of the procession, so late that we had missed the welcome drink (Guinness or Harp lager served in pint paper cups – an innovation).

The refreshment caravan, with its head start, was set up and as we arrived at the first stop each of us was handed a welcome pint – this was consumed with ease. The weather was hot, we must guard against dehydration, the creamy black liquid slipped down soothingly, its bitterness cutting through the mucous of exertion. We had a second. Then off we set on the next nine miles.

The physiology experiment had failed to include any study of the diuretic effects of alcohol which was a grave omission. We were thus unprepared for the effect on our fluid balance – the balance between how much of the ale contributed to our hydration compared to how much it subtracted by making us pee behind bushes. What we did know was that by the time we staggered up the hill to the second refreshment stop we had a prodigious thirst!

Had we been better prepared, at this stage we would have quaffed water (which may even have been available) or better still, a dilute electrolyte solution... But Hell! Guinness must contain some electrolytes.

What happened next starts to become a little vague. I remember sitting on a wooden field-gate with Ruth. A silver vintage car drove into the next field. Someone said, 'That's Gus Campbell – he's in our year.' We looked up and both toppled backwards off the gate and into the long grass. My head described a perfect arc and at its highest point my eyes recorded the distant image of a small (because it was a long way away) open top silver vehicle driven by a black dot – it was the black dot that I would eventually marry. I did not know this at the time, so it was not a big deal!

Soon after this we stepped out onto the next stage of our journey, Ruth, Fergal, Jiggery (who wasn't strictly a medical student – but no-one asked, despite the fact that he was having an inside-out day) and me. Fergal was in our year and had been away with a group of us in the Easter vac, he had bought Jiggery with him who wore his clothes the right way out only every-other-day – he had been to the same Catholic boarding school as Fergal and now manufactured greetings cards. We walked arm-in-arm for stability.

We were amongst the last by the time we reached the next official stop due to having had an unofficial stop at an unknown hostelry, only to use the lavatory, but we couldn't do that without having a half. The official purveyors of refreshment were eager to get to the last stop before the winners came into the finish. They may also have felt some duty of care. Anyway, they poured us several pints to take with us and bundled us stragglers, well – staggerers, into their caravan – 'is this safe?' – and set off.

They stopped abruptly several hundred yards from the finish and unloaded us into some bushes. 'You stay there until you have counted at least ten men and three women go by – do you understand? It's one thing cheating but we can't have you winning.'

'Absolutely not!' we all agreed.

'Might it help,' asked Fergal, 'If we took our beer now?'

'No!'

Thus abandoned, we hid in the bushes to count runners. We were amazed at the focus and determination that we saw in the front runners – the entire purpose of the enterprise appeared to have escaped these ardent athletes. However, counting blinkered-over-achievers is rather like counting sheep; very soon all four of us were deeply asleep.

When we awoke it was because Fergal was shaking us, he had woken first and gone in search of, amongst other things, a lift home. He had met some chaps (I use the word advisedly) from Guy's who could drop us off in Plumpton where Jiggery's parents lived. Fortuitously, Jiggery's parents were also away on holiday and the key was always hidden in the garage – it was essential for us all to make haste to the Guy's mini-bus as soon as possible. This we did. It was dark now, but we found it parked in a side street as painstakingly described by the chaps. We climbed in carefully so as not to spill our drinks (one for now and one for later) There were no windows and no seats but no matter. We sat on the floor and propped ourselves against the sides of the vehicle. Ruth lay against a pile of blue coats. She was asleep almost immediately and soon we had all nodded off – we had, after all, walked three-quarters of a very long way.

'Hallo... Hallo... What have we 'ere?' He really did say that – the large police officer who opened the side of the police van to reveal four bodies.

There was no blood and closer examination revealed signs of life. My eyes had opened the instant the officer had flung open the door and my hearing was intact but my motor functions were strangely impeded. I could only turn my head slowly towards the officer and blink. His helmet left little doubt as to his identity.

'Is this not the Guy's minibus then?'

'It is the Sussex Police van.'

'Oh.'

'Shit! We're going to have to find those Guy's chaps pretty damned quick or we'll lose our lift!' said Fergal gathering up his cigarettes which lay beside him.

'Hang on a minute,' said the officer, now flanked by two amused colleagues. 'It's 11.30 pm, we're packing up, pretty well everyone else has gone… You've been had, mate!'

'How on Earth are we going to get to Plumpton now?' I asked, shaking Jiggery who did not respond.

'What's… Where…' said Ruth

'It's okay Ruth – there's been a bit of a misunderstanding.'

'Plumpton's just West of Lewes, isn't it?' asked one of the other officers, 'It's not very far out of our way. Our HQ is in South Malling, just the other side of Lewes – you are in luck!'

Just after midnight, assisted by the Sussex Constabulary our group, now quite wakeful after our nice rest, broke into Jiggery's parents house where we fired up the record player and danced until dawn.

At this time, I thought we had just climbed into the wrong van and did not believe that the boys from Guy's Hospital Medical School had played a trick on Fergal, an oik from the women's college. Neither did it occur to me that the same Guy's men might have been entirely mythical and that we all might have been tricked by Fergal into engineering a lift home from the constabulary. Getting to know him better would raise many such doubts.

Chapter 13.

Student life – bullying, and fighting

The summer term was packed with physiology and biochemistry, with notebooks full of pages of formulae as human biochemical pathways were recorded and, perhaps for an instant, grasped. This was the very end of the era when everything you'd ever need to know was taught – we even had a short course in thermodynamics (an understanding of which underlies the understanding of almost everything). However, try telling that to the average medical student who knows he will not be examined on the subject!

The Professor of Thermodynamics was a world-class scientist, he had a German accent and probably a Nobel prize. Unfortunately, he was not a gifted communicator and there was something about him that turned a Victorian lecture theatre with its circular tiers of normally attentive and good-humoured students into a bear pit. Our Freudian friend, the head of student health, would have done well to use his lectures to demonstrate the pathogenesis of bullying.

The key in this case seemed to be disengagement (failure of the students to grasp what he was saying, initially due to his accent, volume and the complexity of his thoughts). This was followed by lethal student boredom which provoked the odd diverting and amusing comment. These comments, initially made as quiet asides, were seized upon by the tiers of suddenly and uncharacteristically under-stimulated brains. The disruption was contagious, it became amplified as responsibility was diffused. Group dynamics came into play and a hint of traditional medical arrogance (who does this guy think he is that he can waste our valuable time!)

Soon everything the Professor said was met by hoots of derision. For those who were not carried along by it, this was really quite scary, the more so because it was so easy to become amused and drawn into the hilarity. One or two of the older students got up and left as the poor professor tried to soldier on. He scurried back and forth behind his desk, head down, not making eye contact, writing formulae feverishly on the black board, expounding quietly his mind-blowing truths to the remaining hateful students – frantically he cast his pearls before swine!

The Royal and Ancient was different from other medical schools. It was less conservative, had fewer traditions; perhaps it stereotyped its students less. It had more women students, more mature students, more foreign students, more students who were just plain odd – it relished diversity (which had not yet been invented).

When I went there, I expected, if I had any expectations at all, that the other students would be intelligent, well-educated and highly motivated, generally like myself, only more so. This was not the case.

My first year at medical school was a great revelation. In those days, at that institution (at least) some of the students from very grand sounding public schools, ones you have all heard of, seemed to me to be very poorly educated. Perhaps the more prestigious medical schools had creamed off the best of their students.

I did not consider myself a musician, but I had learned to read music at junior school and was shocked to find that this was not the norm. Many of the students came from private schools and their parents, like Ruth's, had spent thousands of pounds on their education and some hadn't even learned to swim.

Students, it seemed, were a hugely mixed bag and, as time went on, I started to recognise patterns.

I would wonder why some students spent so much time doing things other than medicine. There was the concert pianist – a boy who was nearly always in the Junior Common Room playing the grand piano that someone had donated – he played extraordinarily well – he seemed more like a concert pianist to me. As it happened, he also came top in most of the exams.

There was a girl who lived in a large flat in Kensington with her parents (both doctors). She hardly ever attended the medical school – she was busy doing what debutants are supposed to do. One afternoon she took a group of us home for tea, perhaps to show us the vast social chasm with which she was having to cope. The butler served Earl Grey tea from a huge silver teapot while the housekeeper handed out hot toasted teacakes from a matching antique chafing dish. One of our number was the son of a successful East End car dealer (they now lived in a huge house in Hampstead) but he was Cockney through and through (and very bright). As we all departed this lad grasped the butler by the hand and shook it vigorously, addressing him as if he were the father of our hostess, and thanked him heartily for his hospitality. I suspected that he knew very well what he was doing!

This girl had known exactly what she was doing too, despite the growing suspicion that she had a complete lack of enthusiasm for actual patients she subsequently chose a niche speciality, largely administrative and non-clinical in which she soon rose to the very top. She had had a strategy all along!

There was a lad with a Dutch-sounding name who had black fingernails and spent most of his time in the little garden of the house that he and his friends rented. I visited it once – there was no earth visible in the garden, a narrow path divided the thick verdura, of fourteen varieties of salad plants, planted in blocks of different colours, greens, purples and red. Each variety had strips at different stages of development. An English salad at that time was defined as undressed lettuce, slices of cucumber, segments of unripe tomato and a dollop of salad cream. He proudly showed me his three varieties of endive, his crisp white chicory, the lollo rosso, radicchio and red chard. I recognised the beetroot and the spinach but had never seen them grown as a salad. I tasted rocket for the first time, it was quite new to Britain. Behind this salad-carpet of flags-of-all-nations he grew all sorts of unusual vegetables, Jerusalem artichokes, fennel and broccolis. Behind them were vertical pipes with holes cut in their sides for herbs, wild strawberries and trailing nasturtiums.

'Don't you grow any potatoes?' I asked.

'No, not even on the allotment. I grow mostly asparagus, globe artichokes and flowers there… And make my compost. I only grow premium crops that I can sell to a couple of restaurants and a florist in Mayfair –they take pretty well everything I can grow – it pays for the beer!'

'Where did you learn to grow things?'

'At home, I suppose… My Dad grows orchids.'

'But you've got such a talent – what on earth are you doing studying medicine?'

'I ask myself that! Would you like some of these little tomatoes –

they are very sweet – I got the seedlings when I was in Holland (new F1 hybrids) and I've got them under cloches.'

I was starting to feel that I might have a genuine vocation for medicine when I got to know so many other students who plainly had not. There are many motives for studying a subject, as many motives as there are people probably. What worried me was the number of my fellow students who did not really want to study medicine, maybe didn't even want to study anything.

I was fascinated by these wayward students (usually boys) channelled by teachers or parents (some of whom I noticed were schoolteachers themselves, but more often doctors) into a difficult, challenging career for which they had little interest and often no aptitude, or obviously more aptitude for something else – for example the gardener and the chap who fixed his own car so that he couldn't drive it when he was drunk!

There was another boy, really young, only seventeen when they let him in as an undergraduate, whose parents were both eminent members of the profession, or so it was said, and evidently both quite elderly. They probably wanted him off their hands before they retired; people said that they wanted him quickly qualified to take over his mother's very profitable society practice... Who knows!

He was tall, a strange, quiet, pale boy with curly ash-blond hair – he smelled of tobacco. He had a friend (a boy who had gone into medicine on the back of his sister – a past gold medallist). At weekends the two of them would drink themselves into a frenzy of antisocial behaviour. They threw a crate of bananas through the window of the corner shop, they borrowed cars and smashed them up. They fought violently with each other, terrifying their flat-mates and girlfriends and quite seriously injuring themselves, each other and anyone who joined in the brawls or tried to separate them. They broke windows and doors with their bare fists, and they would go on drinking until they lost consciousness and became comatose. It was a miracle that neither of them came to serious grief at the time.

They were not bad boys, he and his friend – they spent a good deal of the rest of their time making reparation, mending doors and windows, repairing the dents in cars, suturing each other's lips and buying bananas. The other students seemed to consider them entertaining – characters!

This notoriety did not help them. They did not help each other. This was, after all, what medical students were supposed to do – be wild and drunken – work hard and play hard!

No-one intervened, took them aside when they were sober. No-one pointed them in the direction of the Freudian lady or even a wise GP. Yet every one of their friends would come to understand that this behaviour was seriously disturbed, but not quite yet.

One of them made it through the eye of that needle through which young people have to pass – but only after several years of psychiatric treatment and with much co-lateral damage. The young man with the ash blond curls died by his own hand soon after qualifying.

I studied hard. Well, maybe not hard, but consistently. I had never been a swot but did feel increasingly privileged to have the opportunities that I did have. I was state educated and was now supported by an adequate grant, to which my father made a modest contribution, and I was a woman. I knew that if I did not make the most of my opportunities it would impact on other women, those that would come after me.

It seemed that Fergal, with whom I was now loosely, romantically connected, had a completely different approach. Trying to fathom this exercised me considerably.

He hung around the medical school and chatted to other students, perhaps he studied in secret – he had no books. He had come from a school run by monks – presumably very strict, probably didactic – had he never had to find anything out for himself – did he not know how to study? Perhaps he was like a woman I knew, who thought if you mixed with sporty types, or clever people, or beautiful people or the rich, you became sporty, clever, beautiful or rich. He would become a doctor by magic osmosis. Some people, I was beginning to realise, could not grasp the concept of *cause and effect*.

Fergal was charming and amusing. When pulled over by the police for driving his moped along Gower Street late at night and very drunk the police officer said, 'Sir, have you been drinking, you seemed to be wobbling?'

'Officer, I find that remark offensive, I may be as drunk as a skunk – but I was not wobbling! I never wobble!' At that point he dismounted and toppled into the gutter. The officers, amused, picked him up and dropped him off at the Catholic Chaplaincy having first helped him chain up his moped and put the key safely into an inside pocket.

Fergal was like a stage drunk. 'Uncommonly decent of you!' he said to the officers in his deep, lilting voice, shaking them warmly by the hand then waving them away while staggering incongruously up the Gothic steps – he could win anyone over.

He stayed at the Chaplaincy. That is probably not to say that he lived there or paid rent – he may have done at some stage. I suspected that he had thrown himself upon the charity, ignorance or gullibility of the Holy Father's subordinates in London. Fergal certainly knew his way around the Catholic Church and (somehow) the Navy – two closed shops that ordinary folk did not usually understand. He had obviously hung around with priests and sailors, much as he now hung around with medical students. Such knowledge is inordinately useful to the sort of person who sails through life on a wing and a prayer. You can always procure a reference, a letter of recommendation, a certificate of attendance or a note from the friend of a friend of a friend from one of these secret worlds. Genuine or forged, no-one will pursue its origins through the corridors of the Admiralty or the Vatican.

He had long, unruly, frizzy hair of a gingery-brown hue and at that time a matching, equally unruly, beard. Despite his youth, this bizarre hair growth, extreme thinness (due to a combination of borderline starvation and chain smoking – the last being responsible for the first), and the affected speech of an elderly, Jesuit monk. Fergal neither looked nor sounded young. At the age of nineteen he had assumed a persona that could take others a whole lifetime to perfect.

But, for all that, there were certain strange imperatives in his life. His year was marked by certain, almost sacramental, events. I might have just about heard of Henley Regatta or Cowes Week, but they were of absolutely no importance to me. Fergal could not miss them.

That year Fergal insisted that I bought, for more money than I could really afford, the right sort of dress. No boy had ever supervised my choice of dress with such a bizarre interest nor referred to some tribal dress-code. This was particularly peculiar in the context of his own accustomed state of dishevelment. The next thing was the picnic – for a young man who took not the slightest interest in food it seemed odd that he should become so pathologically pre-occupied with the picnic hamper. I bought or borrowed a large wicker basket with handles and lid, not absolutely conventional for it was round, but Fergal was satisfied with it. He then listed the statutory contents – a French baguette (which would poke out in the required fashion), Camembert, dry white wine, Pinot Grigio or (better still) a Muscadet, and strawberries.

'But I prefer a red wine with bread and cheese!' said I, who was interested in food.

'Muscadet!' insisted Fergal. 'And a blanket to sit on.'

So, on a sunny day in July, we were to be seen strolling along the riverside path at Henley's famous rowing regatta, looking for somewhere dry to sit, I getting my heels stuck in the soft turf. We did not have a programme and did not enter any of the enclosures but Fergal, who had donned his old school blazer (that had seen better days) and battered boater, pointed out the boats belonging to specific teams, the colours of which he recognised as they flashed and grunted past. Fergal may have nodded at one or two people but spoke to no-one.

A little beyond the course we found a suitable spot and ate our picnic.

Later that summer we did something similar but less elaborate at Cowes, sleeping in a tent and consuming Guinness with some young people that Fergal knew, a considerable amount in Fergal's case after which he became uncharacteristically affectionate but far too affected by alcohol for mortal sin. However, we had experienced a certain closeness, in that tent, and I felt it was a sort of breakthrough. Next morning Fergal was agitated and upset, and it became clear that he had no recollection of the previous night and was very afraid of what he might have done.

This amnesia hurt me and made me angry and I punished him by not telling him, ever, what had transpired in our night of passion.

That summer we went on holiday together with Mireille, my French penfriend and Phil, another friend of mine from home who had got to know Fergal on our Easter trip – he was up at Cambridge.

We took my parent's notorious and ferocious green tent to Dorset – it was obviously male as it responded well to Mireille and my gentle coaxing approach. The boys slept in a smaller borrowed affair that leaked. Phil was learning to play the guitar and Mireille had perfect pitch and a beautiful alto voice and large repertoire of folk songs. It was like being on holiday with Joan Baez [6]. I had a harmonica and Fergal looked the part.

'Show me the whisky stains on the floor, show me the drunkard as he stumbles out the door,' we sang. 'There but for fortune go you and go I.'

Every evening we drank cider in a tiny pub and sang songs. The cider was nine old pennies per half and had a kick like a mule (more than thirteen pints for a pound!) The locals did not seem to mind our intrusion, probably because they had been consuming the local cider in large quantities for many years.

Mireille and I did not drink very much of it but I soon appreciated its pharmacological potency when I noticed that I had developed a generalised, though painless, urticarial rash – the funny thing was that I didn't have it where my clothes had been, my shorts and sleeveless T-shirt were clearly visible, printed as normal skin on my otherwise red and blotchy body.

'When you fell over and rolled down the little hill you touched something *nuisible* you are *qu'est-ce que c'est, allergique*,' said Mireille who was not a medical student.

That afternoon we retraced our steps of the night before, along the footpath from the pub and found the large area of flattened stinging nettles in the ditch where I had rolled, giggling, the night before! This understanding of the anaesthetic properties of alcohol would stand me in good stead in the future when called upon to suture the lacerations of hopeless and irritating drunks. I was never cruel, but I knew I could safely omit the trouble of a local anaesthetic!

That was also the day that I learned something else about drunks – they lose things. I discovered that my wallet was missing – we thrashed the nettles, but the nettles would not or could not give up the missing article that had contained my last ten shilling note, a letter from Fergal

6. *Joan Baez – folk singer from 1960s – particularly associated with protest songs.*

in which, to my surprise, he said that he loved me, and nothing else – life was simpler then.

Losing the money was not a disaster, we were going home the next day. Mireille, Phil and I were catching the train together back to the Home Counties. Mireille and Phil still had enough money for a taxi to the station. Fergal would use his trusted moped to not wobble (he never wobbled) back to his hometown on the Solent. The disaster was that, however hard I tried, I could not dispel the thought that Fergal might have taken my wallet. He almost certainly had not (I knew I had been drunk because of the nettle bed incident) I could have lost it anywhere. But what I did know was that I did not truly trust him. It was unthinkable that the other two could steal from me, but it was thinkable that he could – even if he didn't – and he probably didn't!

The closer I got to him the less I seemed to know him. '*Show me the alley, show me the train. Show me the hobo who sleeps out in the rain.*' We used to sing, '*And I'll show you a young man with so many reasons why.*'

The following term I stopped seeing Fergal. I told him the truth. I did not want to invest my emotions in a relationship with someone who arrived home in a police car not knowing where he had been or what he'd been up to. I couldn't live my life like that. I was not Catholic, but I felt sure that God would not accept 'not remembering' as an excuse for anything! I told him I had a nagging fear for his future – I could all too easily see him as a vagrant, a tramp, a homeless, chronic alcoholic.

He probably never forgot those words. And I – well, I thought they were my own, but I never found out what were the so many reasons why. Not much of a friend really was I?

He failed his exams and the next lot and then he disappeared – another drop-out?

He was not stupid – far from it and he spent so much time hanging around in the cloakrooms of the examination halls listening to the hysterical rantings of the students who had just been examined that he must have picked up the answers to a lot of *frequently asked questions.* And never underestimate the power of his charm!

In those days you could still get a licence to practice medicine and surgery from the Society of Apothecaries or, as you still can, from the Royal Colleges of Medicine, and of Surgery. You had to pass an examination and have evidence of study at a recognised institution, a note from the dean of your medical school, a letter from a Surgeon Commander in the Navy perhaps or the Reverend Mother, Doctor Annunciata Maria of the Religious Sisters of Charity, St Vincent's Hospital, Limerick, if there is such a person, God bless her, or such a place.

This was the back door into Medicine and (which ever door he went through) I found out decades later that Fergal had made it into the profession and was practicing as a junior anaesthetist. It was said that his practice was basic but careful. He labelled his syringes 'sleepers' and 'wakers' so as not to get confused – that sounded like Fergal!

Chapter 14.

A testicle on a plate

By the end of our pre-clinical studies Ruth and I had adjacent single rooms in the hall of residence. Our rooms overlooked the roof of the theatre next door that belonged to RADA, the Royal Academy of Dramatic Arts. We spent a good deal of time at our desks which were placed to afford the best view from the window. This was both distracting and diverting.

Like many old buildings in London, the roof of RADA was inhabited. The theatre school overflowed on to its several different levels – ladies in long robes and mediaeval whimples would promenade, arm in arm, lost in conversation – a couple would fall repeatedly into each other's arms until their clinch was completely satisfactory to the third party watching from the level below or thoughtful young men would strike poignant poses while learning their lines. But mainly the activity was sword fighting!

I had fenced at school – I had been Girl's Junior County Foil Champion for which I had a very small gold medal – very few schools did fencing at that time! I knew enough to realise that RADA took their fencing very seriously. Occasionally they would cavort with a fencing master in masks, the instructor shouting out the required moves in French but rather than performing, for that was what they were doing, on a straight piste, these students fought in three dimensions using the whole mountainous roof. This involved considerable choreography and jumping about. The young men swashbuckled about the roof, leaping from level to level, battling up steps and flinging each other over backwards before one of them died horribly and I would fling open my window and clap. That is when I would realise that Ruth had also opened her window to wave at the young men in tights.

'Get your head down Miss Benedict!' I said to Ruth as we both hung out of our windows.

'Half an hour on the brachial plexus then I'm off out – are you wearing your Mum's red Crimplene shift tonight?'

'Yes, are you wearing your long red Wellies?

'Not if you are wearing the dress... I'll toss you for them!'

'I'll come round.'

Both of us withdrew. I had taken up the hem of the red dress that I had purloined from Mum. It was tight on either of us, but we both loved it. Ruth's long red Wellington boots, bought for riding in the rain, were not really the correct specification for dancing all night but were more comfortable than heels and (in 1969) had exactly the right look with the dress which exactly matched. Part of the deal was that the boots, which smelled appalling when not plugged up with a tightly fitting calf, were stored at all times in their owner's room. Tonight, Ruth won the toss.

It was getting towards the end of our 2nd MB exams – Ruth was still revising anatomy as she was expecting to be deferred in that subject – she had (she was sure) failed her recent viva. The impenetrable Dr, now Professor, Tweed had offered her a gnarled and pickled object on a white dinner plate – for a moment she had been puzzled, unsure what to do with a pickled walnut.

'Describe!' he said.

'It's round... well oval... I mean ovoid.' She gave its approximate measurements.

'And this?' he asked pointing with his little, silver pointing stick to a stringy thing emerging from one side.

'Is attached...'

'Yes'

'She peered through her thick glasses. 'It appears to have an artery and a vein... Perhaps more than one, and there is some sort of duct.'

'Yes... Ring any bells?'

'Kidney! No... No, I know, it must be an adrenal gland.' Ruth was panicking now.

'And does that have a duct, Miss Benedict?

'No. It's a ductless gland.'

Ruth had picked it up, held it in her hand, she had felt the weight and still she had failed to recognise it.

She was devastated after the event. 'On a plate...' she kept repeating. 'On a plate... Me! And I didn't know a testicle on a plate!'

Now, the reason Ruth wanted the red dress that night was that she was meeting her new boyfriend, Brad, an American PhD student from Imperial College.

'If he comes back with me, I'll pop the boots outside your door.' We both knew the reason why.

Next morning I fell over them as I made her way to breakfast – I never missed a meal however bad I felt in the morning but today I ate alone. I encountered Ruth, uncharacteristically animated, peering furtively from her slightly opened door.

'Pst! Di!'

'Hello!'

'Can you pop round the corner and make sure the coast is clear then go to the stairs and stop anyone coming along here for a moment or two, while I get Brad out onto the fire escape.'

'It's daylight, you know.'

'I know – we overslept!'

'Morning Brad!' I nodded to the head looking over Ruth's shoulder, 'This must all seem very strange to you.'

'For Christ sake, she's twenty-three and I'm twenty-seven! What is it with you people?'

'Ruth might be old enough to look after herself, but you might want to rape and murder the rest of us! They have to protect the innocent! I'll check the corridor.'

I went to the main corridor and signalled that all was clear and paused for a moment to see Ruth bundling the young man and his belongings, including a rolled umbrella, towards the back stairs with the half landing which gave onto the Victorian fire escape. Then I went to the main stairs to way-lay any chance witnesses – there were none.

The following day Ruth announced that Brad had rung her – there was a large noisy pay phone just outside our rooms. It had taken him ages to get through as there was always a queue of girls waiting to use it during the day. He wanted to take her to a trendy restaurant in Chelsea the following Saturday (she was excited) and he was offering his fellow PhD student, an Englishman, to deal with her innocent friend.

'Thanks!' I said with irony.

'It'll be fun!'

'It'll be the most sophisticated thing I've ever done,' I said, without enthusiasm.

'I'm not sure he'll be all that sophisticated.'

'I meant the restaurant!'

'So, you will come?'

And I did... And he was not very sophisticated. He was not just English: he was Lancastrian. In his late twenties, he had shoulder-length mouse-coloured hair, clean but dishevelled and not in a trendy way. It seemed that the object of the evening was to challenge my innocence and that this young man had in some way been appointed envoy from the Sexual Liberation Front. This interested me, I wanted to know more – I cross-examined him (it was always my way). Before anyone knew it, I had uncovered his early sexual disasters, his shot gun marriage to a girl at school, his impending (allegedly) divorce, his two children (estranged – allegedly) and his poverty (undoubted). His nervous tic got worse and worse as the evening progressed. We finished our over-priced beetroot soup with sour cream and a bread roll (with poppy seeds) and he drove us back to our hall of residence in his old banger.

I became aware that I was sitting on something uncomfortable, I groped under my coat and pulled out a one-eyed rabbit (a toy, not a real one).

'Ch... Ch... Chuck it in the back.'

I did so, accidentally glimpsing what would be my image of *the swinging sixties* on the back seat. I was not shocked, just surprised by my friend's suppleness and vigour. I looked quickly back to the road ahead – it was already 1970.

Next evening the phone outside our room was ringing insistently – no-one answered it. Eventually I got up from my books and answered it. It was Brad.

'I'm sorry Brad, Ruth's not in. Can I get her to call you?'

'No, no, Roo told me she was going to meet her sister. It's you I wanted to talk to.'

'About what?'

'I just thought I'd like to get to know you a lot better – I wondered if you could drag yourself away from your books to have a drink with me? I'll be free about six.'

'Hang on a minute. You know that I am Ruth's friend – she is a very good friend and I happen to know that she is very keen on you –as I think you must know.'

'That, as they say, is her problem – not ours. How about it?

'What sort of friend do you think I am? Get lost!'

I put the phone down and wondered if I should tell Ruth – there didn't seem any point, she would find out soon enough what a shit he was. However, when Ruth was trying (unsuccessfully) to contact him in the ensuing days I did say. 'I don't know why you are bothering –he's just a bastard American who thinks he's God's gift to women!' But Ruth knew that already – that was her problem.

'I don't know why I bother with men like him... Well, I do... But I shouldn't... And meanwhile all the decent men are being hoovered up... I think there's only one eligible man left in our year.'

'Oh yes, and who's that then?' I asked.

'Angus Campbell.'

'Is that the chap that you spoke to on the stairs yesterday, queuing for the refectory? With the pipe and the old tweed jacket that's too big for him?'

'That's him!'

I would recall this unsolicited reference the following day, and at many other times in my life, and wonder if it was that remark (the last eligible man) from the friend (famed for her poor judgement of men) that had tipped me over the edge.

This was a time when history was happening fast. I knew this because of David Hendry. He was a friend of my parents – he had just telephoned (he was to be in London after Easter and wanted to see me). He was younger than my parents but older than me. He'd been to Oxford, got a blue, went into the Guards, then into the Colonial Police in Africa where he'd risen rapidly. After independence of his emergent African nation, he had stayed on to coach the national team for the Commonwealth Games. Then he had 'retired' at a ridiculously young age with sunburned knees and immaculately parted black, Brylcreemed hair to pursue his hobbies of photography and writing. I never saw anything he had written (nor any photographs for that matter). He was single and kept himself very fit, always lived abroad and moved around quite a bit but came home every year or so and always visited my parents – I assumed he had a crush on my mother but also wondered about his sexuality – perhaps the attraction was my dad (that made me smile).

He seemed very unlucky in his choice of ex-patriot dwellings – within months of moving anywhere the newsreels would start rolling – there would be political unrest, uprisings, kidnappings, coups – all within weeks of David's arrival. Bearing in mind that the BBC in those days had relatively little coverage of things that happened abroad, it seemed that David had a knack which might have made him a great war-correspondent, of being able to exactly predict the next trouble spot.

He had started his 'retirement' in a villa hanging with wisteria and old vines in Famagusta in Northern Cyprus. No sooner had he unpacked the telephoto lenses for his new camera and fitted a new ribbon to his typewriter than the constitution of the newly independent state, which had been carefully negotiated to protect the Turkish minority, started to rankle with the Greek majority and the president. Within a couple of years David must have watched it all unravel – although he never told any of those that he visited in England about it. Soldiers appeared from mainland Turkey and there were Greek air strikes and soon David moved on. He never gave anything of himself away when he talked which always seemed to me to be in riddles. They were not ones with an answer but ones just to make you think he was clever and that he knew what you did not. The timbre of his voice had a strange metallic ring, an urgency, a command, a dominance, and the slightest remnant of a Scot's accent (like the first James Bond) – I thought he would be good with dogs. I fantasized about him coming home one day from Jordan, or Yemen, or Zimbabwe and seducing me.

Now he had made contact with me in my second year at medical school – he would be staying with his brother for a couple of months, he gave me the number. 'When you are back after the vac, give me a bell and we'll get together for a meal – you're not in some ghastly relationship, are you?'

I assured him that I was not.

But first I had to cross the Rubicon, in my knitted miniskirt and Mum's red jumper and with my reading glasses firmly gripped in my hand. I had to jostle my way through the other students to where the results were posted, in long lists which were pinned to the wall of the long narrow corridor by the Registry.

I shouldered my way through the throng of agitated students – the greatest fuss being made, it seemed, by the ones who had passed – one large girl who had done rather well, sinking to the floor and sobbing in a heap, presumably of relief but preventing others from being able to get to their results. Histrionic high-achievers jabbered and squealed their complex primate behaviour with quasi-concern and ritualized embracing.

The lists of names were ranked with those with the highest marks at the top and the lowest at the bottom – the pass mark was a horizontal line about three-quarters of the way down – there had been a record number of failures.

I was in the top ten for everything. Ruth was delighted (but did not jump about) – she had passed everything except anatomy and in that she had only a modest deferral and would be allowed to resit after Easter. She would go home, deliver lambs by night, bash the books by day and with luck be able to go on to Clinical after the Easter break.

That night, before we all dispersed there was a hop in the Junior Common Room. Ruth and I were to go together but just as we were locking our doors the phone on our landing rang – it was Brad.

'You don't mind, do you?' said Ruth. 'But it's the only opportunity I'll have to see him before I go, he says he's been trying to get hold of me for a fortnight!'

'Go on then!' I said in that flat voice that my mother used when she disapproved but knew she was beaten.

So, I went to the hop on my own. The JCR[7] was full of people but the band were having a break and I could see no-one that I knew – there were lots of halls of residence in the area and students from other colleges often attended the medical school hops. I edged my way to the bar which had steps down to a sea of bodies none of whom were familiar.

The first person I did recognised was Angus Campbell, puffing his pipe calmly in the midst of the throng, 'Hello Angus. How did you get on?' I shouted over the din.

7. Junior Common Room

'Passed! And you?'

'Passed too!'

'Well done!'

'Well done you too!'

'I don't seem to know anybody here.'

'What did you say!'

'I don't know anyone!' I shouted in his ear. 'Are you going to the bar? Would you mind getting me a drink – I'll never get there in one piece.' I thrust a ten-shilling note at him that I had ready in my hand. He took it and disappeared, and I stood uncomfortably in the corner near the door being jostled by those trying to get in and out.

Eventually he returned, edging his way through the noisy crowd, leading with two wet, slopped half-pint glasses of beer.

'I'm afraid they are half-empty!' he shouted.

'Half-full!' I shouted back, smiling...   And that is how it would always be.

*

That night he took me home to his horrible little room in Camden Town.

When he had moved in at the beginning of that term, the inventory had listed the linoleum, a small table (Formica slightly damaged), kitchen chair, single bedstead and mattress, fitted cupboard, coat hook, two coat hangers, one electricity socket, a pair of cotton curtains and one net-curtain with wire. No lamp shade was mentioned as there was none, nor had there been a bulb in the single light- fitting that dangled from a plaited brown and frayed flex to be hazily reflected from the dirty window where the unpullable nature of the curtains allowed it to shine dimly out over the walled and bramble filled rear garden.

Angus had unwrapped and fitted his light bulb, filled his kettle from the grubby wash basin in the toilet on the half-landing, plugged it into the single electric socket and unpacked his chipped mug, teaspoon, bag of sugar and tin of Nescafe and his life in London had instantly been re-established after the previous vacation.

At the beginning of every term, he did exactly the same thing but in a different depressed area of the city in another rooming house close to the tube.

It is strange that I did not interrogate Angus on the subject of his appalling living conditions – that in itself was out of character – it might have revealed valuable information. As it was, we had more important things to do. We had both passed 2nd MB, I was three months off twenty, here was a nice young man and there was one big hoop that had to be gone through! Timing in life is everything.

Chapter 15

Life and Death

The next morning I left early, but not before extracting certain commitments from my lover. My breath billowed in the chill air and a milk float rattled past parked cars from under which cats scuttled homeward as I made my way to the tube station. My parents were to pick me up at Hall, with all my stuff (I had considerably more than Angus) and transport it home for the Easter vacation.

I had promised to look after my granny for a few days while Dad took Mum away for a rest and, he hoped, a bit of attention for himself.

Back at Hall, I bathed and took satisfaction in the first sign of my period which I was expecting that day... Perfect. Just before 9am I was seated in the waiting room of the Student Health Service surgery in Gray's Inn Rd where I acquired a prescription for the newly available oral contraceptive and an additional bag of assorted conventional contraceptives (condoms, including coloured and flavoured versions which were another example of the hard-nosed business acumen of the pharmaceutical industry in its bounty to medical students).

I also received numerous leaflets and various spermicidal concoctions. Armed with this heavy burden of protection, I strode out of the building with new confidence, straight into the path of the Dean of our medical school.

'Out and about early this morning, Miss Grant – I thought you'd all still be celebrating – but then perhaps you have been?' she said with a quizzical smile and clinical insight honed over many years which, this bright morning, fixed on my lips and chin.

'Absolutely. Good Morning Doctor Bagshott.' I nodded deferentially and turned abruptly into the adjacent graveyard to scuttle through the grave stones oblivious to the spring flowers.

In the chemist's shop in Marchmont Street I surrendered my prescription and my mental stability in exchange for three small packets of pills. I also bought some foundation cream to cover my stubble rash and made haste back to my room to apply it before the arrival of my mum and dad.

I need not have worried – my mother was far too excited to notice anything. She was, of course, pleased that I had passed my exams but what really exercised her was the prospect of three days in a hotel in Broadstairs.

Granny was now ninety-three and lived in the house that she shared with her son, my uncle, Peter, in the same small town in Hertfordshire where my parents lived. Granny had been in rude health but had, a few months previously fallen over and fractured her hip. The surgery had been successful, but her general health had been undermined by the trauma, the general anaesthetic and one or two mini strokes – even the cerebral ischaemia of that decade reflected the spirit of the age! These events had undermined her general health, cognitive powers and confidence but not her good humour.

Her bed had been moved down to the dining room and the dining room table and chairs now sat incongruously in her bedroom breathing in the scent of lavender and Vick.

On either side of her bed, midst a slight but distinct odour of roast beef (the effluvium of decades of Sunday lunches) – was now parked a Zimmer frame and a large mahogany commode. The processes that we all take for granted, when we are young (getting out of bed, passing urine, opening our bowels, wiping our bottoms, washing our hands, dressing, cleaning our teeth, eating, wiping our mouth) now suddenly came to the forefront of Granny's world as if wanting their just recognition, waiting to take their final bow. From being almost unconscious acts, they had become the whole object of life in that house.

And for poor Peter, now in his sixties and always inclined to avoid unpleasantness and to scrub himself violently twice a day with carbolic soap, this organic assault on his sensitivities was intolerable.

He scuttled past the door to the dining room holding his breath, took his bottle of whisky from the base of the grand-father clock and withdrew to his meticulously clean and tidy garden shed – to place his cut glass tumbler on the scrubbed deal slats and savour the scent of drying onions and rose fertiliser made from the ground, dried, but sterile bones of dead animals.

Granny's care was left to my mother while her brother pretended it wasn't happening. Now that my mother was close to collapse, I was to take over the management of these bodily functions for my grandmother for four days and three nights, the district nurse would pop in each morning.

Something strange had happened – I was nineteen and three quarters and I had crossed a watershed. I had passed my exams (none of which related to the care of the elderly), I had come home from university and was now to be left in charge. Okay, it may have been one of the longest childhoods in history, but it seemed to have suddenly ended. Within forty-eight hours something invisible had shifted and I had stepped into adult life.

Over the previous few months Granny had borne her disability with humour. As I now wrestled to insert her into robust and unco-operative support stockings to stop her legs from swelling to three times their size by evening, the old lady lifted her other leg admiringly from the bed, looking at the morning trimness of the ankle and said. 'Thank Goodness I've never lost my good legs!'

Once dressed Granny was manoeuvred into the sitting room where Peter could talk to her through the French windows and where she could watch Eamon Andrews on the television. 'I see they've got those blue flowers again.'

'It's black and white, Gran – the doctor says it's your eyes!'

'I don't know about that, but Peter's got them in his shrubbery too. Oh dear, I need to have another wee – can you get me up.'

'I'll bring the commode in here – we can pull the curtains.'

'Don't be silly Dear – there's no-one in the garden. Just put the tea towel over the television.'

'They can't see you – you can only see them, Granny.'

'That is all very well for you to say – Cover him up!' So, Granny wee'd while Eamon Andrews went on talking with his soft Irish brogue, tactfully pretending not to notice the tea-towel over his head. Tellies were much smaller then.

*

Prior to this time, every few weeks the old lady's confidence would falter, 'You had better send for Diana, Evie – I think I might be going to die tonight.'

This had happened two or three times – it had unnerved Evie. I had, on each occasion, arrived home later in the day to the great joy of my Grandmother who then announced that she was feeling very much better and would like a small brandy. After this she would loudly question what all the fuss was about and send us all away.

On the third night of my custody of my grandmother it came to the old lady's notice that she had not seen her daughter for some time. 'Call your mother, Dear. I think I might be going to die tonight.'

'Mum will be home in the morning – shall I get you a little glass of brandy?'

'Ooh! Do you think that would be a good idea?'

'Yes, I think so, Gran – it would be medicinal.'

'Medicinal?'

'Oh yes, definitely medicinal! It's very good for the circulation.' So, Granny had her brandy and slept well. She did not die in the night.

The following day, according to plan, my parents arrived back from the coast, Mum looking youthful and pretty, Dad looking almost relaxed.

There was just time to get me to the station to catch the 12:05 to King's Cross. There I walked the short distance to St Pancras tube and got the Circle line to Paddington and comfortably caught the train to Taunton.

Meanwhile, having discharged his duties as Best Man at a friend's wedding, near Barnstable, Angus was making his way, from the opposite direction by car.

The train was heaving with people: busy, cheery, outward looking individuals, all with their own tumultuous lives, all caught by chance in the belly of the same creature as it hurtled westward.

A young man gave up his seat to an old lady who rummaged in the strange, knitted portmanteau that she had placed on the table in front of her. We were crammed into one of the new carriages with double banquettes facing each other across tables. The old lady pulled out a packet of custard creams which she opened and proffered to the young man and to the other passengers, those opposite, over the piled baggage and those standing in the central walkway. The packet was passed over heads and under arms that supported those trying to keep their balance as the train thundered through Farnborough. 'Ooh, don't mind if I do!'

Life stories were exchanged between all these complete strangers and in no time at all they were disgorged at Basingstoke or Andover to resume their own particular narratives: to fall weeping into the arms of their mother or to shake the hand of a prospective father-in-law or find a taxi to a bed and breakfast, to be ready for that job interview in the morning. These were the days of social intercourse with strangers – when your own good mood could bounce about those around you in a public place. Moments of communion were created where today there is only forbidding space.

Forty years after this day on the train, one of my daughters will chastise me on the platform of Paddington station for 'making too much eye contact'. 'When you come to London you have to allow people their own space – stop trying to engage people Mum, you'll get yourself into trouble … Or everyone will think you're barmy!'

Forty years earlier no one had minded the old lady with the custard creams. She had been an icebreaker, a facilitator!

Angus was uneasy as he sped along the A38 towards Taunton: the car was running well but the cable brakes on his renovated 1936 open-top tourer were not adjusted as they should be. Every time he put his foot on the brake pedal, he could tell it wasn't right, the car pulled to one side. He really needed to adjust them.

I erupted from the train onto Taunton station on a wave of optimism. I looked both ways but saw no one. I walked out of the station and looked both ways. In the distance I recognised the silver form of an open car – I walked towards it. As I got closer, I could see its polished chrome headlamps and the red hood folded back. Angus was sitting in the driver's seat puffing his pipe. 'Chuck your bag in the back,' he said as he leaned over to unlock the passenger door. I climbed in, smiling broadly and kissed his cheek. He turned the key in the ignition. We were on our way!

300 yards from the station there was a level lay-by, Angus had spotted it on the way in. He pulled into it and stopped – I was gratified. I linked my right arm with his left and gently pulled him towards me and we kissed. 'Would you mind doing something for me,' he said to me as I looked deeply into his eyes. 'The brakes need adjusting, if you could just sit in the driver's seat and work the pedals, I can manage it, it's nice and flat here.'

Before I knew it, he was out of the car and had got his tools from the boot and was lying with his head and shoulders under the car shouting directions to me, 'Brake! Release! Brake!'

Thus, was established the pattern of the holiday, indeed the pattern of our life together – he would have a smouldering pre-occupation around which I moulded my life... Quite happily.

We motored from quaint fishing village to quaint fishing village in a stuttering, guttering, pulsatile way as Angus used each stretch of straight road to test his brakes, every flat lay-by to re-adjust them and the next stretch to re-test them and all others to re-assure himself that they were working correctly or, indeed, to re-awaken his concerns.

In the evenings, with my gold-plated brass wedding ring (from Woolworths) in place, we booked into a bed and breakfast, sought an evening meal on foot, and retired early to bed. This part of the day ran more smoothly – the nights were blissful. In the mornings we rose early as was the custom in 1960's B&Bs, ate cornflakes with creamy milk and lots of sugar, a full English breakfast and loads of coffee with toast and marmalade – we needed it.

Thus, we wended our way from Beer, which was a place with sea gulls and church bells, to Looe where we encountered the mother of an old school friend of mine with a man that I assumed was her husband, a colleague of my Dad (though I had never actually met him before). I swallowed hard and thrust my deceitful left hand into my pocket and advanced with my right outstretched to shake their hands. I had been carrying the bags out of the guest house, Angus was bringing the car round. The other couple had emerged from an adjacent building, also with bags. Pleasantries were exchanged. Angus drew up at the curb and offered to give them a lift to the town car park down the hill, they declined. 'Remember me to Polly!' I said as we parted.

'That just goes to show!' I said as I climbed into the car.

'Shows what?'

'That your sins will find you out!'

'Yes. I thought they looked shifty,' said Angus with a flash of insight.

*

In Cornwall we visited derelict tin mines perched on cliff edges, the water crashing below – Angus knew all about them. He had a brother, four years older – a black sheep. It was he, it seemed, who had the obsession with tin mines and their father, eager to engage the boy, had taken them to all the tin mines he could muster. These expeditions had taken place on family holidays to St Ives – Angus took a detour to show me the hotel where they had always stayed –it was large. Their mother had not been there, she had flown the nest many years previously when Angus was still a baby.

Brother Rod had visited most of the mines since, without his father, and been down most of them.

'Are you allowed to do that?'

'I shouldn't think so – but then that wouldn't bother Rod. He can't resist exploring mines or caves – he's a potholer. And he collects engines, steam engines. He must have re-built his Land Rover four times – it's water-proofed so that it can drive through rivers and it's got a winch that runs off the engine and arc lamps mounted on the roof.'

'It must be wonderful to have an elder brother.'

'Not really, we 've never seen much of each other – we didn't go to the same school. Rod was always getting thrown out of schools.'

'Why?'

'I don't know – I suppose he was thick.'

'He doesn't sound thick!' I said sounding almost indignant.

'Perhaps he just wasn't interested in what they wanted to teach him.'

'I've heard that said about self-made millionaires who left school at fourteen because it was such a waste of time when they had so much that they wanted to get on with!'

'Maybe that's right,' said Angus. 'But it was hard on Pop – Rod was always a worry to him.'

'Is Rod the reason you re-built this car? Did he help you?'

'No. Dad and I did this after Rod left home. Rod was never interested in doing anything with me –four years difference in age was a lot – he didn't want me hanging around him. Anyway, it was probably bad enough for Pop having one wayward son, without him dragging his little brother into danger.'

Angus told me that his brother had made a bomb one day from the innards of fireworks and set it off, remotely, in a well that they had in a mock Tudor folly in the garden – it had gone off with an unbelievably loud bang and blown the heavy iron cover right off the well and deposited it at a considerable distance, nearly demolishing the folly. The story was told with great enthusiasm and it was clear that Angus was considerably in awe of his brother.

Despite this one episode, I got a picture of Angus's childhood, at home, as rather isolated and lonely – a big house, a father, a housekeeper and an elder brother more often conspicuous by his absences. Boarding School, he claimed, was happy. 'Well, not exactly happy, but alright – we got privileges as we got older – we had our own cubicles… And if we got bored we could always go and spy on the girls at the Ladies' College!'

That was where we went next – to look at the austere buildings in Cheltenham where Angus had spent many years and to see the gap in the hedge where boys, who were destined for Parliament, the Judiciary, Medicine and the Church, jostled to get a view of girls in short green skirts playing lacrosse!

Holiday over, we did not quite part. I took him home and my mother made a great fuss of him and as he lay on an old sack under his car on their driveway, Dad operated the brake pedal for him. We slept in single beds in separate rooms. Then he drove me down to Surrey to meet his father before we set about finding him some digs for the following term.

Now that he was embarking on his clinical studies, he needed to be near the teaching hospital. I had already arranged to move into a double room with Ruth in a large flat rented by my friend Jane's elder brother (an entrepreneur) who sub-let it to as many students as he could reasonably fit in, mainly ex-Cambridge graduates like himself – all eminently eligible but too late for me now. Sexual pairing was, I was learning, mainly a question of timing.

The plan was that I would, indeed, move in with Ruth and the nice young men from Cambridge (a bad enough prospect for my parents) and Angus would get a bed-sit nearby with a double bed.

This we did. On moving day (the Sunday before the start of the new term) I waved goodbye to my dad, who was anxiously parked on a double white line then I carried my boxes of books and files and a small suitcase up to the flat which was on the fourth floor of an Edwardian block now owned by the Council near the Heath that had no lift. Ruth had already moved in with a whole term's worth of stuff. There was very little space in our room.

After a welcoming mug of tea from a handsome medical student from Bart's and a trainee accountant, I said. 'I think I'll just pop down to South End Green to see how Angus is getting on, I might stay the night, I'll take my suitcase, so I've got clothes for the morning.'

The following week the trainee accountant was kind enough to drop in with my boxes which Ruth thought I might need. I paid the rent on our shared room for three months after which time Angus and I told my parents and the medical school of our change of address and we moved to larger rooms belonging to his land-lady's friend around the corner.

Angus and I did the introductory course to clinical with pathology, pharmacology and bloodletting together. Then, as Angus progressed to the wards, I took a year out to do a BSc in Physiology –this was what more able students were expected to do and having had a good look at the other students in my year, that was what seemed appropriate. It also put a year between me and Angus so that the pressures would be staggered.

My parents, who were terrified by the new arrangements, figured that if (in the worst possible scenario) I were to become pregnant and have to give up my studies then I would at least come away with some sort of degree. I had no intention of becoming pregnant.

This was a time of anecdotal medical teaching, when doctors shared, and valued experience rather than computer verified evidence, of which, of course there was none. One of the first facts that I learned in this way was that if you put a dried pea into a jam jar every time you have sex in the first year of a relationship and then, in subsequent years, you take one out every time you make love – your jam jar will never be empty. That first year Angus and I put a lot of peas into our metaphorical jar!

I would not get a first in my BSc, but I got a valuable breathing space to adjust to adult life and, when Granny really was dying, I could go home and lend a hand.

My mother and I sat either side of the old matriarch's bed, one on the seat of the commode, the other on the convenient flap-down seat of the mark II Zimmer. Each of us held one of Granny's hands. Geoff, my father, was pottering in the kitchen. Uncle Peter was sitting in the shed, his elbows on the aforementioned, scrubbed deal slats, slumped over the cut glass tumbler, his eyes moist and inflamed.

Granny slipped out of life without any fuss, with just longer and longer pauses in her breathing and at the end of the last pause a little twitching so that, for a instant, both of us started to rise thinking she wanted something – then nothing, she was gone, and we sat back and looked at each other.

Now, in the last few months, as the old lady had become weaker and the nursing heavier, Evelyn and Peter had engaged the services of a private nurse who came every morning and took over for a couple of hours. She had come highly recommended by Granny's doctor and had become, she said, very fond of the old lady. She was a tall, lean, upright lady who had retired as a senior sister at Guys Hospital to look after her own mother who had recently passed away. She wore a smart blue uniform with an elaborate silver belt buckle and starched white cap with white ribbons that tied under her chin.

She would assert the importance of respite for carers dispatching Evelyn to the kitchen for cups of coffee and to town for essential items of quality care for the elderly including enormous rolls of cotton wool, castor oil, rubber gloves and KY jelly, zinc ointment and air fresheners. Large cardboard boxes of incontinence sheets arrived from the Red Cross and insinuated themselves into Peter's shed. Sheepskin booties for heel care were sought from farther afield and blocks to put under the feet of the bed and under Granny's chair. All Granny's nighties had to be split up the back to just below the shoulder blades (and hemmed) for ease of access – she certainly knew what she was doing. 'When the time comes,' she insisted. 'Whatever the time of day or night – you must phone me, and I will come and do the necessary – at Guy's we were taught to see things through to the very end.'

Neither I nor my mother knew what exactly 'the necessary' was, under these circumstances, but ever dutiful, we did as we were bid.

At ten o'clock on a Friday night, just after we had phoned the doctor to tell him that Granny had died, we telephoned the nurse.

Half an hour later the doorbell rang – I opened the door. There under the large square canopy of the porch, illuminated from above, stood Sister Catchpole in uniform – well, not quite in uniform. Her white hair, normally pinned back tidily, was dishevelled, her cap was crooked with the ribbons dangled loose and flew about in an agitated way when she moved. The top button of her tunic where the starched white collar should have been attached was undone so that the collar stuck out on one side, as if indicating, and those lower buttons that were done up were out of step, left with right. Her belt was only half hooked so it sat askew. Her shoes, I noticed, were not quite a pair and her stockings were twisted to such an extent that Mum who was standing in the doorway to her mother's room found herself wondering in alarm about the state of her suspenders.

At this moment Peter came out of the kitchen to see this paragon of twenty-four-hour care in the community advance into the hall with a strange and wobbly gait.

She caught her brown shoe on the edge of the door mat, but her body continued its forward trajectory, her feet now running to catch up, she pitched forward into Peter's arms. 'So sorry,' she rasped, her head pressed against his chest, 'for your loss.'

Peter, bewildered, set her upright and left – heading up to the grandfather clock on the landing where he kept his spare bottle. She stood very straight for a moment and put her hands to the sides of her head as if to smooth her hair and feeling her cap, straightened it then turned to Mum and said, 'I shall need a basin of hot water, clean towels and cotton wool.'

There then ensued a strange ballet. The sheet that had covered the deceased grandmother was whisked away with the skill of a magician or a matador. I expected Granny to jump. 'I can do this alone if you prefer,' said the artiste.

'No, I think I had better stay…' I said. 'To learn.'

Mum was not so keen. 'Well I'm going to put the kettle on and wait in the kitchen,' she said.

With great aplomb, Sister Catchpole proceeded to teach me the laying out process. Throughout she held a large roll of cotton wool under her left arm and after each statement, rather than doing what she had just explained, she took a handful of cotton wool and cast it onto the scene – like a flower girl with petals. The dissertation seemed absolutely correct – perfectly drilled into her at an early age but the actions came from somewhere else entirely!

Enough was enough. I went for more hot water. 'She's as drunk as a skunk!' I said to my mother and the man with the stethoscope, who had just come in the back door. 'It's a good job Gran had a sense of humour. She's toppled over twice – the floor is awash and the whole place is a snow storm of cotton wool!'

'This is fun!' said the doctor. 'Like an Irish wake. I'll have a look at the body then I'll take her home – Sister Catchpole that is.'

Mum and I stood in the porch watching the doctor manhandling the nurse into his car, then he picked up his bag and carried it to the boot. That was the moment that I recognised him – it was Polly's dad with whom we'd had the embarrassing encounter in Looe – only it wasn't her dad (who was an engineer) was it? It was Granny's doctor.

Chapter 16.

'Raped, buggered and bewildered.'

The old hospital had sheds on the roof and some of the sheds had other, smaller sheds on their roofs. These were linked by rickety walkways and ancient wooden steps where the pigeons roosted and laboratory technicians sat on sunny days having their lunch and where it was said, at night, male students were seduced by Night Sister.

One of these sheds up an unsound flight of steps was today set out with rows of wobbly folding chairs, perhaps enough for forty students. Angus and I sat in the front row, only one other chair was taken – one other student was nodding off in the second row. That was what happened when lectures in non-examination subjects, however tempting the title, were scheduled for 9 am on a Saturday morning towards the end of term! The lecturer was none other than Sir Francis Camps, the Home Office Pathologist, renowned for his interventions in high profile criminal cases over the previous thirty years. He was coming to the end of a distinguished career and doubtless wanted to share some of his hard-earned wisdom with those starting out on theirs – to forewarn us of some of the pitfalls – to disabuse us of any naive notions we might have about human nature. He had, through his work, plumbed the depths of human depravity, fatal carelessness and breath-taking bad luck. Week-in and week-out he had seen the results of do-it-yourself electrical wiring, drunk driving and illegal abortions, presented on his slab. He had been a staunch supporter of the campaign to legalise abortion, the law on which had finally been liberalised in 1967 and the effects of which were only now starting to improve matters.

Francis Camps' evidence had been crucial in the prosecution of the multiple murderer and abortionist, John Christie at 10 Rillington Place – the notorious case where the murders of two of his victims, a mother and small child, were blamed initially on the woman's husband and father of the child who was hanged for their murders. This was long before other bodies were discovered in the garden of the house they had shared with Christie and which were eventually to hang Christie.

This was despite the fact that when the garden had first been searched after the disappearance of the mother and child the broken fence was propped up by a human thigh bone that the police failed to notice. This case, along with other miscarriages of justice led to the abolition of capital punishment in the United Kingdom as recently as 1965.

I was shocked by this lecture – not by the revelations of three decades of brutality, sexual perversions, abuse and corruption but by the fact that so few of our fellow students had thought it a worthwhile subject for their attention. Many of them would end up as psychiatrists, paediatricians and family doctors (some even police surgeons) and would confront, first-hand, cruelty and neglect. I felt forearmed, primed to be suspicious, unashamed of being alert to inconsistencies. Throughout my subsequent career I would record the core temperature of any corpse that presented itself to me, unless it had been in the fridge for hours. I would examine the neck for fractures and run my fingers through the hair– looking for small calibre gun-shot wounds that might otherwise go unnoticed and other evidence of foul play. I never signed a cremation form without stripping the body and turning it over (which was to make me very unpopular with undertakers).

It was not long after this lecture that poor Professor Camps died, not long after marrying his third wife. The fact that she was a toxicologist (a world authority on poisoning) seemed to amuse Angus – nothing about his death was in the least bit suspicious but the way we looked at things had altered – he had left us with a legacy of suspicion.

During the Introduction to Clinical Studies, Angus and I were in the same set of students, the course was to last three months and included Pathology, Pharmacology (the working of drugs) and a half day's tuition on blood taking.

During this latter exercise, students were paired for practice and Angus nobly volunteered for me to take his blood. Now I was not particularly squeamish – on the contrary, I was keen. I felt for his vein (distended by a tourniquet) cleaned the area with spirit (to make it sting) and inserted the needle into the vein (it was surprisingly sharp and easy). Then I withdrew the plunger of the syringe and this was the part I was not prepared for – fresh blood swirled into the syringe and triggered a very primitive reflex – my blood pressure dropped, I paled,

I wobbled, the syringe parted company from the needle and Angus's life blood flowed down his arm and splattered onto the floor promptly followed by me.

'Here we go!' said the demonstrator, leaning over and pushing a cotton wool ball onto the entry site and pulling out the needle. 'Bend your arm!' he said. 'Leave her, she'll be alright – her head is nice and low – if that had been her blood it would have stopped flowing by now –see how shut down her peripheral circulation is!'

All Angus could see was his new love, crumpled and white on the floor – he went to scoop me up, 'Keep her head down', said the demonstrator. 'You don't want her to fit or get brain damage – we really ought to have a couch for fainters to lie on.'

Angus whisked me away out into the cool corridor – I was starting to come round – the blood was still dripping from his arm. Someone opened a window for him, and he draped me, unceremoniously over the wide, stone window ledge with my head outside – he held tightly onto my belt. I felt terrible – was this to be the end of a promising career?

'I didn't vomit,' I said weakly as I sipped a glass of water a few minutes afterwards. Half an hour later, when it was Angus's turn to take my blood, I turned my head away and did not look at the syringe.

I was not the only person to pass out that afternoon, but the episode worried me. The main function of clinical students within the hospital (apart from looking and listening and answering the odd question) was bloodletting. They presented themselves each morning on the wards to which they were allocated and went round taking the blood samples for the tests that were ordered by the Houseman.

The fact that the reflex dropping of my blood pressure at the sight of blood was undoubtedly an evolutionary advantage was no consolation. My primitive ancestors had survived all manner of accidental injury, lacerations and stab wounds without exsanguinating due to this ability to lower the pump pressure of their circulation to produce the merest trickle of blood loss while playing dead (as I had done). Their assailants flushed with success beat their chests and ran off to pick on someone else.

Times had changed and I did not intend to spend any more time than necessary with my head stuck out of windows or vomiting into fire buckets – I had a plan!

I had a four-week gap before starting my BSc – I scanned the local papers and there it was – 'Wanted – *Temporary Phlebotomist at the Soho Hospital for Nervous Diseases. Training given – terms and conditions on application.*'

Each morning, early, I rode my bicycle across Soho Square as the sunlight crept between the buildings with their faded grandeur, flaking stone finials and withered acanthus leaves. As the sun defrosted their outer layers, the vagrants in their many over-coats and long tangled beards were stirring on the benches and the last of the working girls were clicking their high heels briskly in the chilly morning, past old King Charles on his plinth looking as worn and pitted as the poor old tramps. Around the mock Tudor folly, the pigeons pottered, turning over fag-ends and pecking at litter. Even the pigeons were scruffy and defeated –– not the plump, iridescent, air force blue ones of Trafalgar Square, these were thin, charcoal grey and moulting.

The Soho Hospital was a crumbling homage to Victorian beneficence, and probably guilt, it was slap bang in the middle of the Red-light District, a stone's throw from Soho Square. If ever there was a building whose damp basement should house someone who collected other people's blood – it was this one. In its core was an ancient elevator, like a lion cage with long loops of cable that hung down and moved ominously up and down as the lift creaked and rattled its ascent and descent. Its iron trellis doors grabbed at the corners of white coats as they tried to leave and no one in their right mind would travel in it – very few of its passengers were in their right mind.

As it was no longer the time when *any man worth his salt had a positive WR* [8] (Wasserman Reaction for Syphilis) cases of General Paralysis of the Insane, which had been the hospital's bread and butter, had dwindled to a couple of cantankerous old ladies sharing a room on the top floor. The hospital now majored on tragic cases of Huntingdon's Chorea. The iron bedsteads on the wards, largely unchanged since Victorian days, vibrated with the un-coordinated movements of men and women, some related – affected by this

8. *Said by Sir George Qvist, Senior Surgeon, to. any number of students*

autosomal dominant condition (if one parent has the disease there is a 50% chance of inheriting it). The laws of Genetics were difficult to work out before DNA studies, family tree studies were frequently muddied by misconceptions (literally) about paternity. Before 2003, unless you had a dimpled chin like your father or characteristic crossed front teeth (like me and my dad), it was difficult for anyone to be absolutely sure who their father was – in view of human nature this was not necessarily always a bad thing.

It soon became apparent why this small hospital needed a full-time phlebotomist (gatherer of blood samples) and that my risk of fainting was not to be my greatest challenge as most of the patients had dementia and extreme difficulty in controlling their movement. A request to *roll up your sleeve* could result in wild flailing of the arm in question or a scuffle as the patient scrambled to get *under* the bed. One patient lived permanently *under* his bed where I crawled dutifully about my duty. Often the more a patient concentrated on trying to keep his arm still the more extravagant would be the movements. Speed, accuracy and distraction were the key and extreme concentration on the job in hand such that all primitive reflexes were suppressed. I did not faint once, nor stab myself with a syphilitic needle, and would eventually enter my clinical years confident in this one area.

Chapter 17.

Academia and the military.

A few students each year stayed on in the pre-clinical medical school to study for an intercalated honours degree in a pre-clinical subject. I had chosen to do this in Physiology and, like most things at the Royal and Ancient, it was a fairly relaxed affair. Students chose specialist subjects and then with one or two like-minded students decided on a subject for research, read what other people had done, then devised themselves a research project. The medical school provided them with the necessary resources, advice, assistance and licenses. It was a tremendous opportunity for a curious student who wanted to test herself, or himself, in a research setting.

Now one thing you don't already know about me is my long and chequered relationship with God. When, just before puberty, I had announced that I was to be confirmed in the Episcopalian Church I had been miffed when my father had for one of the only times in his life, put his foot down and told me I was too young and must wait until I was older. Thinking about it all at that time made me feel very unfaithful to God and guilty at which point I deduced that I must have been brainwashed by my mother and the established church. What I would do was *take a year out* from believing, pretend there was not a god, thus un-washing my brain so that in a year's time I could consider the whole matter again in an objective fashion! Poor God never really recovered. However, I could not easily break my promises – even to a discredited deity. When my paternal grandmother (who suffered with her nerves) had become so ill with an anxiety neurosis that she spent months in hospital and ended up having brain surgery I had (aged about seven) entered into a pact. If God made Granny's pre-frontal leucotomy work, I would dedicate my life to neurological research which was odd because it long pre-dated any ideas of studying medicine.

Thus, came the God-given opportunity to start my life's work with a year's research including modules in neurophysiology!

That particular year none of us got a Nobel Prize but we demonstrated for ourselves the amazing homeostatic abilities of the mammalian circulation – it was reassuring to find the myriad ways (other than fainting) in which the body compensates for blood loss. We amazed ourselves with the knowledge of just how hard the mammalian heart could pump, a good lesson to learn at this stage in our careers. We were forced to mountaineer on an industrial stepladder to clean the blood off the high ceiling lights of our lab. I had let slip my grip on a cardiac cannula causing instant red-out as blood sprayed our goggled eyes blinding us temporarily and turning the whole place pink.

We investigated how thyroid function is regulated, learning tedious bio-assay techniques and then took our results down to the immense computer in the basement to work out just how significant they were. We cannulated microscopic vessels in the mesentery of living tissue (making our own glass cannulas) then fiddled with the flow of the tiny pink doughnuts that are red blood cells as they whizzed about carrying oxygen. We tinkered with the neurones of giant squid although we never met one personally.

This truly was the end of another era – when science was do-able, all you needed was a notebook, a pencil, test tubes, a few chemicals, glass rods, copper wire, rubber tubing and a battery. Given an oscilloscope and a smoked drum, the sky was the limit! This was how all the great medical discoveries of the past three hundred years had been made. Everything, as I said in the beginning, was changing. Science, and more particularly – technology, was on the march – soon it would all be different.

Did God keep his side of the bargain? Well, he did for six weeks – Granny became serene. What was demonstrated most clearly, was the miraculous power of homeostasis in systems (even the brains of grannies). In the seventh week Granny's brain had found new ways to connect so that it could send its anxieties around new circuits, could again wring its hands at the imagined infidelities of her husband and her imminent abandonment. Intelligent, middle aged, middle class women, who after the war went back to sitting at home, too posh to do anything and waiting to be side-lined by a mistress, frequently became unhinged.

At Farnborough, in Hampshire, the Royal Air Force had the Institute of Aviation Medicine. At that time, they were keen to recruit young (male) doctors to the service – they lured them to sign away their freedom as students with promises of a smart uniform, regular income, mess dinners, boundless sport and flying lessons. They were not yet interested in female students or lady doctors, but they were sensitive enough to realise that specifically excluding women was starting to be tricky. Thus, for the first time, in about 1971, some women including myself were invited with a selection of likely boys to Farnborough. The students were a select band mainly from London medical schools and from Oxford and Cambridge towards the end of their BSc courses. The system of teaching was relaxed and much less academically exacting – however we were given little projects, real human volunteers to experiment on and some amazing kit to play with. There was a giant centrifuge in which we could spin airmen while making them breathe radio-active gases to ascertain the effects of G-force on respiratory function. One of the much-despised lady students pointed out that the subject of the experiment was a serial volunteer who had a resting respiratory rate of 60/minute. She suggested that this almost certainly indicated some underlying pathology which should preclude him as a *normal subject* – maybe he volunteered all the time because other more strenuous duties were becoming difficult for him due to his deteriorating emphysema and bronchiectasis. He was also, she pointed out, repeatedly assaulting his almost certainly diseased lungs with all manner of toxic substances in the name of science. The wing-commander mumbled something about Crown Immunity and the volunteer disappeared.

Next, we played with the compression chambers – contraptions designed by Jules Verne! These were thick-walled steel containers with portholes and pipes curling around them and a door I had seen in submarine war films. Now the RAF hatched its subtle and cunning plan. They divided us students into two groups and while one group worked the controls outside and observed through the portholes the other group were shut in and alternately pressurised and depressurised so that we could experience the anoxia (lack of oxygen) of altitude and the hyperbaric effects (increased oxygen saturation) of a deep-sea diver. This was not just for the hell of it – the subject students had to complete tasks of dexterity and reasoning. Then we had to look at the results with our academic medical student hats on. This would clearly show which young men they should be recruiting.

In fact, it did not take complex statistical assessment to notice that there was an obvious gender difference – at ground level some of the bright young men performed exceptionally (just as expected), they were quick and accurate, had exceptional spatial awareness, impeccable logic and scored highly for intuition and social skills. The wingco rested his hand on the squadron leader's shoulder and they nodded conspiratorially at one another. Names were noted.

Now the first ever mixed gender group was taken up to the equivalent of 10,000 feet and the tests were run again. There were three young women, including me, and three young men. The brightest of the lads was Crispin, infuriatingly from Bart's [9]. At altitude he started looking up from his task and making silly remarks, the other boys giggled, the girls looked round with interest, smiled, then got on with their tasks. 'They are acting as if they're drunk,' I said to the girl next to me. 'Must be the anoxia.'

'It's better than being drunk!' said the skinny, hypermetabolic Crispin, his speech thick as he rolled off the cushion that he had been sitting on and bumped his head on a bolt on the wall of the chamber.

'Your head is bleeding!' noted Cynthia, the red-haired girl from the Middlesex, looking up from her task. The lad put his hand up to his head then looked in disbelief at his bloody hand.

'It's sticky,' he said. 'I'm bleeding, for Christ sake, I'm bleeding!' He stretched up to hammer on the porthole and toppled over again.

'Has anyone got a clean hanky?' I asked.

'I have a pad,' said Jumaana, pulling out a clean white pad from a pocket in the bodice under her sari.

'Give us your tie, Pete!'

'I can't undress in front of you ladies – I've got to do my sums. Not unless you take something off as well!'

'Tie!' I asserted, getting a tick in the leadership box.

By the time we were back at ground level and the door had been

9. *You remember: 'you can always tell a Bart's man, but you can't tell him much!'said by almost all Bart's graduates nearly all the time. (cf Yorkshiremen.)*

un-screwed, Crispin's head was bandaged with a sanitary towel appropriately fixed with an Air Training Corp tie – the bleeding had stopped, and the young man had absolutely no memory of the events that had taken place. Before their descent from 10,000 feet the three girls had all completed their tasks with no reduction on their scores from those achieved at ground level. The same could not be said for the boys.

This pattern was repeated, although not so dramatically, with the other groups and surprisingly also under hyperbaric conditions when one might have expected the thin, young men with their high brain metabolism to function better with a greater partial pressure of oxygen.

Next, we were all allowed to have a go in the centrifuge. This was lodged in a laboratory as big as an aircraft hangar, which of course it had been. The walls and floor were clad in some sort of impervious, laboratory-type material and it was spotlessly clean. I noticed that someone had left a bucket of soapy water and a mop in one corner – quite lax for military cleaners, still, I thought. 'They probably aren't really cleaners – more likely Russian spies!'

It was with great satisfaction that the wingco oversaw two of the girls as they strapped Cynthia, the first of the girls, (in fact the first woman ever) into the chair in the capsule that was firmly fixed at the end of the 8-meter rotating arm. He told them how to attach the various monitors to her. He then withdrew to his control box feeling very pleased with himself that he had avoided handling her thighs personally – although qualifying as a doctor himself before going into research, his limited clinical practice had always been in the airforce and he had never had much to do with handling the female of the species.

'You might feel a little dizzy at the end, as the thing slows down,' he told her over the intercom.

The great arm of the machine started to swing as the hub rotated faster and faster until the capsule on the circumference was just a blur. The closed-circuit camera focussed on the girl within, however, showed her quite distinctly. She was clearly completing the tasks she had been given on the panel in front of her as the cuffs on her arm and her legs automatically inflated and deflated. She appeared comfortable and alert. As the G-force increased the wingco and the

101

squadron leader watched intently – they were assessing her level of consciousness – her heart rate, blood pressure and a measure of the amount of blood pooling in her legs was also displayed on the screen. They threw each other significant glances – the results were evidently not what they had expected!

Having maintained several G of increased gravity for long enough for her to loop the loop several times and recover herself from a near fatal dive, the wingco turned the centrifuge knob anticlockwise and the spinning arm began to slow. Once the thing had stopped it took Jumaana and I several minutes to unplug Cynthia from her various monitors.

'You look a bit pale, Cyn. Are you okay?' I asked.

'I'm fine – a bit nauseated. It gives you amazing vertigo –best fairground ride ever!'

It wasn't until the first of the boys went into the spinner, or rather – came out, that I realised that the bucket and mop had not been left in error.

After my own turn I understood – spinning round at the speed of sound my body, in particular each semi-circular canal in my inner ear, was in a sort of equilibrium – the spirit level in my head spinning at such a rate that the little bubble in the curved tube was transfixed and stationary. However, once the brake was applied and I slowed down the liquid in the canals in my head did not, it had considerable inertia[10] and whizzed around and round telling my conscious mind that I was rolling over and over – somersaulting forward at great speed. Even with my eyes wide open and knowing that I was securely strapped into my chair, nothing in my senses contradicted this view. I had seen my friends leave the capsule pale and wobbly and complaining that the room was spinning but every ounce of my perception said: 'The room is still there – look at it going round and round you, it is you that is tumbling out of control! My God!' I told myself. 'You absolutely cannot trust your senses!'

This had been a very unpleasant experience – nauseating and disturbing, but in years to come, confronted by patients with extreme

10. Inertia: a property of matter by which it continues in its existing state of rest or uniform motion in a straight line, unless that state is changed by an external force.

vertigo, I would be exceptionally understanding. As the patient flailed at the air trying to get a grip on something or clung to me hysterically, impeding my attempts to insert a pessary into his rectum (or inject him) to ease his symptoms I understood his terror and disorientation.

It was not only the students that were picking up useful information from this course – it was becoming clear to the wingco that, under optimal conditions, the highly specialised male brain could not be beaten. However, under stress, the basic model, the unspecialised female brain, was generally functionally more robust and in certain limited situations appeared to perform more reliably. It was still to be years before women medics were actively recruited to the Airforce. It was twenty years before women were to be let loose in fast jets.

Towards the end of the course, one of the flight officers, who had shown no previous interest in us, invited the male students to have a pint in the mess – this was done with studied casualness bordering on the shifty.

As it happened none of the particular women in this group had the least aspiration to soldier "through adversity to the stars."[11] They had enjoyed the generous course and viewed their exclusion from the under-cover recruitment module with equanimity and amusement.

The Wing Commander had the decency to be uncomfortable with the situation. These men in authority had been reared in a hierarchy, isolated from females. They had rigid notions of behaviour and good manners, imprinted since earliest childhood. They could just about cope with the *fair sex*, in their place – and within their own hierarchy – they knew how to dance with the CO's wife, discuss literature with the Air Commodore's good lady and josh with a prostitute off camp. By 1970 the demarcations in society were starting to blur and, confronted by a *bloody woman*, in the absence of uniform or insignia, they didn't know whether to stand to attention or pinch her bottom. I would come across this later in my career and would recognise their dilemma.

11. 'Per Ardua ad Astra' Latin motto of RAF

Chapter 18.

Should I? Shouldn't I?

Angus had his own problems. Medical School in the late 60s/early 70s was academically challenging – not just that there was a lot to learn but the method of teaching was gladiatorial. Six to ten students would stand around the bedside of a patient and were, one by one, mercilessly grilled by the tutor. Failure to understand a question or to give the exact same answer that the tutor had in his head was met with derision and institutionalised humiliation. Often the encounter deteriorated into a *guess-what-I'm-really-asking* situation. When the student failed to come up with the required form of words the question was thrown open to the rest who either tried to make themselves invisible or scrambled like jackals in a feeding frenzy to give the answer. It was all very competitive, and the pushiest students came to the top.

Angus was intelligent and hard-working but inherently well-mannered – he would have said he was shy. He could not bring himself to join in the bloodlust of the ward round so ended up feeling invisible, under-valued and unacknowledged despite having done the work and knowing the answers. It did not help when his infuriating friend, with whom he always seemed to be paired for clinical exercises and who was boisterous and outspoken would on occasions hear Angus's muttered reply, next to him, and broadcast it as his own. This injustice would roll around in Angus's head for days (possibly for years).

We lived now as a couple in rented rooms in North London. If we stuck our heads out of the skylight, we could see a tiny patch of green in the distance that was Hampstead Heath. We had exclusive use of the top two floors – no bathroom –shared loo on the floor below, for £8 per week, all inclusive (four quid each) so, with an income of £11 per week each, we were quite comfortable. It was the financial argument that I offered to my father who had misgivings about the arrangement.

'Go on Geoffrey! Tell her!' urged my mother. Geoff wrote his misgivings (if that is what they were) to me in a letter and posted it to the new address. I recognised his handwriting, placed the missive (unopened) on the tiled, 1930's mantelpiece where it remained for several weeks. When Angus pointed out that I had not opened my letter I moved it (unopened) to my knicker drawer where it would remain (next to the lavender bag that Granny had given me) for many years. I did not feel I could read it as I suspected it might voice matrimonial regrets of his own which I did not feel I could bear. Many years later, tired of looking at it, of turning it over and over in my hands and feeling guilty, I burned it – still unopened.

Later still, after my father's death, I felt even more guilty and wondered what imperative information he had committed to paper, what it was that he could not say to my face – what it was that he thought he had told me and which, because we never spoke of the letter, he then assumed that I knew. Did I have a half-brother in India or a half-sister in Australia?

Meanwhile, this confidential information lived calmly in the aromatic darkness of a drawer on the top floor of a South Hampstead villa.

Two floors below lived a quiet lady in late middle age, she worked at the BBC and had lived there for many years. When first introducing ourselves, we mentioned that we were both students at the Royal and Ancient.

'That's a very good hospital,' said Miss Solomon. 'I go to a special clinic there myself.'

'Which clinic is that?' asked Angus.

'That's what it's called: The Special Clinic. It's written on a big blue sign over the door.'

'Oh,' said Angus, confused and wishing he hadn't asked. 'Must be off.' That is the trouble with euphemisms, he thought, they prevent people from understanding what's really going on – not that he imagined much could have been going on with Miss Solomon – she looked about the last person in need of a venereologist.

We would see her only rarely – her doors were always tightly shut and if she was ever caught accidentally coming or going between her rooms when Angus or I were on the stairs she would open the door just wide enough to escape, sliding silently from the landing and allowing only the tiniest glimpse of her cluttered and faded plush interior.

The landlord and his talkative wife lived on the ground floor with a depressed whippet. The landlord suffered from Chronic Obstructive Airways Disease with frequent exacerbations when he became seriously ill and often had to be admitted to the teaching hospital around the corner. Angus and I noticed that these exacerbations were associated with a distinct doggy smell as we passed through the ground floor and up the stairs. 'Haemophilus canis!'[12] said the infuriating friend, who had seen the Landlord's pathology form at the hospital and had recognised the address. Henceforth all three of us would be able to diagnose this pathogen (to the amazed admiration of our colleagues and our own students) without recourse to laboratory tests – except, of course, to confirm the cleverness of the infuriating friend.

The dog was never treated – we were not that clever, but Angus discovered that his ears (the dog's), which he wore pressed tightly to his little round head could be made to rise slowly to the vertical by bringing a piece of chocolate equally slowly close to the end of his nose. Pulling it away again lowered the ears to their normal position. Eating the chocolate (the dog) also resulted in immediate deflation of the auricles. This was the only sign of emotion that could be elicited from this vector of disease and could be repeated any number of times (size of bar permitting) and gave great amusement to bystanders but not to the dog – just his ears.

One Friday night, Angus and I were leaving for a weekend in the country. As we went downstairs we met Miss Solomon, our downstairs neighbour, coming up with bags and bags of provisions – Miss Solomon had a friend coming for the weekend. She was more animated than usual, which was not animated at all – she had cleared it with the landlord's wife and had bought smoked salmon…

Late on Sunday night Angus and I tiptoed up the stairs having driven back from Surrey in our newly acquired and very ancient Morris Minor. The doors to Miss Solomon's bedsit and kitchen were wide open and, by the light of the streetlamp shining through the front window, we could see that her sitting room was completely empty!

Next morning as I tried to leave for the medical school my way was blocked by the landlady. She was vibrating with uncontainable outrage.

12. Now known as *Haemophilus haemoglobinophilus*, *germ isolated from dog's genital tracts.*

'Disgusting! We're not prudes – you know that – after all, we know you two aren't married – you've been open with us all along and it doesn't bother us at all. But that sort of thing – under our roof. Oh no!'

Oh dear,' I said. 'What on earth has happened, Mrs Plant? What has happened to Miss Solomon?'

'Don't mention her name to me ever again! We had to tell her to leave. Disgusting! Perverted! With another woman! This is a respectable house.'

'But...'

'No buts – we threw them out – there and then.'

'But...'

'Collected her stuff next morning. I locked myself in the parlour until she'd gone... Disgusting!' so saying Mrs Plant turned with a defiant toss of her head and marched to her back parlour leaving me burning with questions that would never be answered. Someone else had dropped out of my world.

'It doesn't seem fair!' I said to Angus that night, 'What is she? Forty-five? Fifty? Living some sort of twilight existence – fantasizing about impossible relationships with equally miserable women. Then two young people brazenly move in together, just above her head and maybe she thought: Why not? The Plants don't seem to be bothered – perhaps times *are* changing... Then Wham! I'd give anything to know what happened that night to bring down all that fire and brimstone from Mrs P.'

'One:' said Angus. 'Life isn't fair. Two: who cares? And three: it's none of our business and... Four, you are nosey – you just can't bear not knowing what alerted the Plants to what was going on and not having the whole story.'

The middle flat remained empty. Miss Solomon's kitchen at the back, where there was an old Ascot water heater, was converted into a half-hearted bathroom – still really a kitchenette with a couple of dining-room chairs wondering where their table had gone and what the yellow bath was doing in their room. Although a source of pride to the landlady, the new first floor bathroom gave no comfort to its proprietor, so much was the anxiety associated with the policing of the same, and the responsibility for switching the boiler on and off on the designated days and the worry about the expense and the condensation and the peeling wallpaper. Angus and I were permitted one bath per fortnight each (not transferrable) with four inches of water (like in the war) on a Tuesday or a Thursday, but only by prior arrangement and with pre-inspection of the water level and with the firm commitment to open the window wide throughout immersion.

Not surprisingly we rarely booked a bath preferring to wash ourselves at our little kitchen sink which was frequently full of dirty dishes and soaking saucepans. Years later, filling up a portable steriliser to boil up some obstetric forceps in a patient's house and struggling to get the cumbersome steel tank under the tap due to all the gunky saucepans piled up beneath it, I would smile to myself, reminded of our first little kitchen. That was where I had started to cook and where Angus had stopped helping with the household chores and where I let him and where I started to feel guilty about the dirty dishes and the piles of un-ironed clothes and where he let me feel guilty and I let him off because he always 'had to work' – as if I did not!

That was where the pattern of our marriage was established, where we went wrong, where I started to let him opt out of anything that stressed him. It had started long before we actually married or had any children. Though I never saw it coming, I colluded in it – I was a victim of my own sexuality and prejudices about how a relationship should be. I wanted to be the best wife I could be, which probably wasn't actually very good. I would try to do 'for him' whatever he needed. I would love him and facilitate his life, the life we shared and in return I knew he would be the best surgeon he could be. And that is what he became but, as a counsellor observed 20 years later, he had not done that for me. I had relieved him of all responsibility at home – he *could* leave and life would go on.

In those early months I would climb the stairs with the shopping or with the clothes from the launderette and think to myself - *Do I really want him? He's not ideal – he is a bit boring – he never wants to do anything,'* and I would answer myself. *'But no-one is perfect, he's decent and straight and honest, he couldn't tell a lie if he tried* (and that was true).

I reasoned that our lives were interesting enough anyway and would soon be even more challenging. I thought that there was a lot to be said in favour of emotional stability and that you shouldn't try to change people – you should accept them as they are and make the best of things. We made love enthusiastically and often and he never upset me (well, not once I had stopped taking the oral contraceptive which fried my brain and made me upset about anything!)

After the first year I seemed to stop having doubts on the stairs but then the Plants had allowed us to decorate and we had painted over the brown, varnished, floral wallpaper with old gold emulsion paint – the colour of sunshine and positive thinking.

Chapter 19.

Clinical

Now there was a problem with clinical studies at that time. The old hospital had been built as a military horse barracks giving it the huge advantage of readymade ramps and doorways tall enough to permit a mounted guardsman with helmet and ceremonial halberd to pass unimpeded. It had been founded to serve the poor and was funded by voluntary contributions and from 1877 admitted women students to study clinical medicine. This was reflected in the very fabric of the place; its blunt masculine stonework being enhanced by the clean, orderly and sanitary precepts of its female staff. The whole place was imbued with the ethos of 'make do and mend.' Thus, it had survived on hard work, common sense and bloody mindedness into the second half of the twentieth century when, as I said at the beginning, everything was on the move again. The old hospital and all its satellites were to be moved to a purpose built, state-of-the-art building, the most modern in Europe (and the ugliest) in North London.

What this meant in practical terms for the students involved was that, until the new hospital was ready, the old hospital would run down even further, maintaining only its renowned specialties (led by such formidable women that no one dared suggest otherwise!) So, the students endlessly interrogated and palpated the same five remaining patients left on the medical ward, all of whom suffered from the rare condition of primary biliary cirrhosis. The excitement was almost uncontainable when one of them developed an ingrown toenail – groups of surgical students came in hordes. On their diet of dark chocolate and maraschino florentines these students longed for the bread and butter of clinical medicine – the phrase 'I've heard there's a case of chronic bronchitis up at Hampstead General,' would empty the clinical common room in the old hospital in moments as a stampede of students, hungry for the everyday, headed north.

Something had to be done. So it was that as the men with hard hats fitted out the new hospital and things fell more and more behind, the students were evacuated to the periphery – sent in groups to distant destinations where real people were really ill. By and large, these students had a lovely time. Enthusiastic, willing, extra pairs of hands were valued in small district general hospitals, they were given lots of interesting, responsible things to do and they got a glimpse of the real world. Many of the male students were seduced by pretty nurses who viewed the sudden influx of potential young doctors as a wonderful opportunity. I was safe as male nurses were still very few and far between and anyway, I was spoken for. I shepherded my three distracted male colleagues around the wards of the hospitals on the south coast where the four of us had been sent. The wards were light and airy and looked out to sea over white cliffs and the nurses wore tightly waisted pink dresses with starched aprons, silver buckles and frilly white caps, they hovered behind bed curtains to whisk them open when they could hear the bedside consultation coming to an end. Then they would smile dazzlingly at the young men as they emerged. Nurses lay in wait to proffer cups of coffee and when asked directions would insist on accompanying the lost boys to their destination while chatting animatedly. All this was to the soundtrack of seagull cries and the voice of Carole King singing from a tape in the Morris Minor that belonged to one of the boys and was our transport for the expedition. Ms King seemed to speak for all the willing, smiling, fresh faced girls in their sunny pink crispness as she reminded them that, *winter, spring, summer or fall, all you have to do is call!*

Richard (the owner of the car, cassette recorder and tape) bathed endless in its sentiments having recently been abruptly rejected by the most wonderful girl in the world – a fact that I was later to corroborate as the girl and I became life-long friends. Now though, poor Richard, though furnished by Mother Nature with all the burgeoning libido that she can summon up on these occasions, was completely incapable of transferring its target, as Nature would direct, from what was no longer available to what was! As he drove us from one sunny infirmary to another *the sky above him grew dark and full of clouds,* but no one called his name.

Fortunately, not all of the everyday London working of the Royal and Ancient was concentrated in the same crumbling and condemned building that the authorities were bent on emptying – some services were in other crumbling and condemned premises but ones whose future was tempered by pressing practicalities and political expedients. 'Obstetrics and gynaecology' was one of these services. Women in labour could not be so easily fobbed off – put on a waiting list or asked to get a referral to another hospital in another area.

Obstetrics and gynaecology staggered on in the Victorian wards of Islington where the poor of North London and the recently arrived immigrants and refugees of the city had long had their babies and suffered the indignities of their gender.

This was a sick institution – its organisation was dysfunctional. To understand this one has to understand that in those days the whole of the NHS structure was based on good will: everyone doing their duty with professionalism and self-discipline (there were no checks, no audits, no guidelines). This made the British health service the most efficient and best value for money in the World. Management was minimal – everyone knew what to do and the management kept their nose out of clinical matters. They paid the bills, repaired the boilers and sorted out the salaries which were not great, but everyone felt that they were an important, indispensable part of the whole.

Occasionally this went wrong (it still does) when no one, outside a department, took an overview or had the authority to knock heads together, or indeed remove heads! Personality clashes, poisonous relationships, occult alcoholism, drug abuse, sexual exploitation, general idleness, or officious over-enthusiasm could and can occasionally affect the functioning of a unit even in the halcyon NHS.

The obstetric service at the Royal and Ancient was one such unit. The medical school (those intrepid ladies at the registry) knew this. It seemed that they had got wind of the fact that it was no place to send high achieving, academic, young women with little experience of the real world. The single women of a certain age (the ones with the Clark's sandals) who worked in the registry would have liked to send all the female students to the Hospital for Women and Children in Paddington Place where the lady consultant bullied the sexually feckless patients but left the students to learn from the patient's mistakes. There were no male registrars to encourage them to learn from their own.

The problem was that there was not enough room for all the girls to go to Paddington Place. They sent the older students, the married ones and the one or two girls who openly co-habited with their boyfriends to Islington. Angus and I had informed the registry of our change of address and the significance had been noted. Thus, poor me, I was sent to the hotbed that was Manchester Street Hospital to learn how to shout 'Never again!' in Greek, in Turkish, in Yiddish and in Urdu.

The underlying sexual tension, between the two male registrars and the body of attractive female midwives, was obvious and not unusual. It was worse than the usual friction between the doctors with the overall authority and the midwives, 'who knew best'. Something about the atmosphere of the place – all the sexually stimulating volatile chemicals swirling around the old, white tiled delivery rooms – the warmth, the poor ventilation, the anxiety. That was bad enough but then add a bucketful of slightly younger, impressionable, single men (the boy students) and a few perfumed young women in leather miniskirts (the 'less vulnerable' female students) and it all got rather silly.

The registrars reacted like threatened silverbacks, beating their chests and becoming overtly sexual with explicit comments and inappropriate eye contact and touching of the females in their territory. The boy students thought this was worth emulating which stimulated the silverbacks even more. A few of the girl students became embroiled in this carnal nightmare, which infuriated the midwives (whether from professionalism, prudishness or jealousy I could not tell). Others became paranoid, angry or depressed (and some probably pregnant) – either way there were casualties.

I watched all this with anthropological interest. I would recognise the syndrome again and again throughout my career. I call it *Doctor's Handmaiden Syndrome*, a problem arising from the other-worldliness of the inside of hospitals. It is where staff find themselves in a parallel, angst and pheromone-enhanced universe – another reality - with work-relationships that can occupy more time and more headspace than their actual partners and families and can become more real.

It rarely ends well.

While the sex-crazed registrars ran the obstetric unit, the gynae side was more the province of the consultants – gynae ward rounds and theatre were sane interludes. Mr Clydesdale was a large, slow moving man who genuinely liked women, he had the persona of a benign grandfather who reassured his patients that a beautiful woman was not complete without a few stretch marks. Miss Pankhurst was Granny to his Grandpa, kindly and non-judgemental, but then she could afford to be – as a Roman Catholic, she was exempt from the new provision of terminations of pregnancy.

She could luxuriate in her knowledge of original sin without the mounting and distasteful demands of the Abortion Reform Act, passed a few years earlier. This allowed termination of pregnancy up to 24 weeks of gestation where there was a risk to the physical or *mental* health of the mother if the pregnancy continued or that there was a risk that the baby or its existing siblings would suffer physical or mental abnormalities as to be seriously disabled. We all have mental health, it varies – mine, for one, was never the same after childbirth! The law was open to wide interpretation which amounted to abortion-on-demand, except in the Hospital for Women and Children in the Paddington Place where it was only available to those who had first been institutionally humiliated (in the name of education).

The third consultant was a small but larger than life woman who operated standing on a small stool, declaiming wildly in an East European accent. She was Jewish and of an age that made me wonder where she had been during the war. No one was ever brave enough to ask her or in any doubt that wherever she might have been it had not been easy or that a lesser woman might not have survived. She had a strength of character, self-confidence and a certainty that deflected any hint of censure.

I watched her deliver a young woman's baby by caesarean section, it was her fifth child, she had four under six years old (two were in care), all delivered in the same way, she was unable to deliver vaginally. She had been warned about the dangers inherent in repeated caesarean sections but still she returned, always in labour, always without having had obstetric care and was always delivered of a normal bouncing baby – always, that is, so far. This time, once the baby was safely out and bouncing noisily, Miss Constantijn asked if the forms were signed for sterilisation, they were not – as always, she had refused.

114

'Oh Dear!' said Miss Constantijn. 'Then we cannot sterilize her that is unfortunate... Hallo, this left fallopian tube is distended and diseased I will have to remove it.' She did.

'Shall I send it for histology?' asked the houseman.

'Not necessary – not malignant. Anyway... Whoops, I have dropped it...And, how careless – I have trodden on it,' said Miss Constantijn. 'But I must check the other tube... Oh dear! We've got a little bleeder here, just by the right tube. Suction please. I'll have to clamp it. Damn! That's torn it. I'll have to tie the whole thing off. Suture!'

In the changing room later I asked the anaesthetist..

'Did Miss Constantijn just sterilise that woman without her consent?'

'That's one way of looking at it... Next time that woman would probably have come in dead... You have never seen a ruptured uterus, I hope you never do, it's catastrophic. She is lucky it hasn't happened already, and lucky she came in when Miss C. was on take![13] Now she might see her children grow up. Sometimes God intervenes, you know, to save people from their own ignorance.'

*

In those days when a houseman took ill or took a holiday his or her place was usually filled by a student locum, usually appointed at the very last minute and selected from the students currently on the firm. This was because scheduled leave always took everyone by surprise, partly because there was no management and because housemen were ever-present and were so taken for granted as to be invisible until suddenly, they were not there. 'Where is Dr Wallace?'

'Skegness, I believe, Miss Constantijn,' answered one of the students on the ward round.

'Well he won't be much use there,' She looked around the semicircle of students gathered by a patient's bedside. 'Miss Grant, you are a sensible sort, aren't you? You had better find a long white coat.'

'Do you want to be a student locum?' translated a registrar in a whisper.

So it was that I became a student locum with all the responsibilities of a houseman without the pay... It was an honour. I held the bleep and worked all day, every day and every other night for two weeks

13. Being "on take" meant taking responsibility for that day's intake of patients.

– clerking all the patients who came onto the gynae ward (mainly threatened abortions, pelvic infections, suspected ectopic pregnancies and women coming in for elective hysterectomies and repairs). I examined their abdomens and their pelvises often surprising myself by what I found – the warm pulsatile mass of my first ectopic pregnancy (and the shocked realisation that my finger should not be there and might cause a catastrophic bleed), the impressive pus of gonorrhoea or a pregnant uterus far bigger that the dates would indicate – I was on a very steep learning curve. I learned how to explain operations to patients in terms they could understand, got consents signed and did the paperwork for terminations. I put up drips and called the registrar when a patient was bleeding heavily or looked particularly peaky. It would look good on my CV and was another example of how the NHS worked – how England worked. Staff could be inexperienced and unqualified but if the boss thought you looked sensible then you could do the job. Nowadays staff must be qualified and have appropriate experience, be screened for criminal convictions and certified in diversity. The consultant's assessment of their competence in the areas required or ability to work with others and communicate effectively when they are actually doing the work doesn't necessarily come into it.

Nobody died while I was a locum.

*

That, however, was not the case a couple of months later when I was doing Casualty and was sent to one of the satellite hospitals in Hampstead to see someone with a quinsy.[14]

Now the one aspect of gynae that had worried me was the therapeutic termination of pregnancy. I could not see how taking a baby's life, however tiny it was, was not an offence, if not against the law, then against Nature. What happened that day would not mitigate that belief but made me realize that there was much more to it than I had thought. I stepped into the entrance of Hampstead General Hospital and could smell it – the unforgettable smell of death.

As I walked towards the casualty department the smell was getting stronger – the smell of anaerobes – the organisms that rot the retained products of conception, in this case the remains of a foetus and placenta, killed and infected but only partially removed by a criminal

14. *An abscess in the throat due to tonsillitis.*

116

abortionist. The mother now being resuscitated in a side room of the department was the same age as me, a student at a London art college. She had the palest, blondest hair which fanned out where she lay, a halo around her white face, as white as the gown she wore. A frantic casualty officer was attempting a cut-down on her wrist, to dissect the vessels in order to put up a drip, so collapsed was she that none could be found otherwise. The girl had walked into the room, the sister had virtually caught her as she collapsed, scooping her up and shovelling her un-ceremonially onto a convenient low trolley (she was only a small sister – only a waif of a patient). With one twitch of her small, experienced nose, the sister knew exactly what was wrong with this poor dying girl and she knew the prognosis. Septic abortions had been commonplace for the first twenty years of Sister Kelly's career. This would be the last that she would see for which she would thank God. Normally a no-nonsense, abrupt sort of woman she held the blond girl's hand and soothed her, stroking her matted hair, laying out the strands radially around her prophetically angelic face while all around her there was fruitless activity. I stood in the corner and watched.

The gynae registrar had now arrived and was in irate but hushed discussion with the casualty officer, who in desperation had moved down to the left ankle in his attempt to obtain a vascular access. I noticed that the wound on her wrist, which lay gaping and abandoned, was not bleeding. The only hope it seemed was to get some fluids and antibiotics into her.

A large priest was getting in the way, removing his overcoat. 'Don't be daft,' I heard the registrar say. 'She can't go anywhere near theatre! She can't even go to the ward – haven't you ever heard of Lister?'

The priest asked for somewhere to place his paraphernalia. 'If we can do anything it'll have to be done here in this side room.' The priest opened his little leather box lined with blue velvet containing a mini, gilded chalice and silver filigree box of tiny wafers, two small cut glass bottles, one for holy water, the other with dregs of wine in it.

'How odd,' I thought, 'It's like a doctor's bag.' In the lid, neatly folded, was the narrow silk embroidered stole that the priest now draped around his neck. The medical registrar had arrived and was inserting a large cannula into the girl's neck. The staff nurse handed him the end of a giving set attached to an inverted litre bottle of plasma. The priest had his little bottle of water in his hand. The girl struggled to raise her head slightly, just for an instant. The priest was muttering '…Lord who frees you from sin save you and raise you up.'

'Amen,' said all the busy nurses without pausing and the girl's head sank back onto the pillow.

'She's gone!' said Sister Kelly, 'You were just in time, Father.'

Chapter 20.

Experience vs. received wisdom

Life, as you will already have seen, often proved to be a surprise to me, and much more complicated than I had been led to expect. Nearly everything I had experienced personally had turned out to be more complicated or more simple but always completely different from what it was supposed to be. I started to suspect this was because those who shaped our knowledge of the world actually knew very little about it. The alternative was that I just saw things differently – marched to a different tune.

Angus was now in his final year. Exams loomed and thoughts broadened to future career and life after medical school – it was scary. The prospect of house jobs, of living apart much of the time and being hugely stressed by onerous responsibility and long hours, all played on our minds. We had both entered this relationship quite casually but, I think, were content. I suspected that reasonable people, prepared to give and take, could forge a good relationship with almost anyone who was also reasonable and prepared to give and take, especially if the sex was satisfactory. I did not have much experience of sex; I had only slept with Angus but suspected that a similar rule applied – if you were both heterosexual and prepared to give and take then you could have a good sex life with almost anyone! Of course, the problem was that there was not enough give and take in the World and none of this quelled the anxiety about our impending change in circumstances. This was a time when we both yearned for something more secure than having shared a flat and a bed for three years. The question of marriage arose, and it seemed just what was required – a stable framework, a foundation on which to stand the rest of our life. That was it: 'life' not 'lives' – one life – together.

Angus passed his exams and accepted a house surgeon's job at a small district general hospital in North London, one that had two consultant surgeons who also worked in the teaching hospital (which still didn't have any patients) but Cricklewood Memorial had wards jam packed with patients – it was a compromise – not a prestigious job but one that

Angus could get his teeth into. Angus would be working for the present and future presidents of the Surgical Section of the Royal Society of Medicine but in their 'other hospital' not their teaching hospital. He and I would marry a fortnight before he started his appointment, and the hospital would give him an on-call room with a double bed.

Cricklewood Memorial Hospital was already an anachronism even in 1973. The main entrance to the sprawling, largely single-storey, red brick building was approached by a modest, crescent shaped driveway. There were railings along the frontage and the way in was flanked by shrubs and a couple of large chestnut trees with squirrels, like a medium sized private house. There was a little carpark for three of four cars and a sign that said, 'Doctors' Parking'. The green front door was newly painted and led into an echoing vestibule with Victorian tiles on the floor and paint or a paler shade of green. Discrete wooden signs with gold lettering indicated the direction of the five Nightingale wards,[15] the Casualty, Path Lab and X-ray Department – that was all because there were no other places to which a visitor might need directions. As you entered there was a small, glazed sliding window to the porter's lodge which was empty as usual except for the distant throbbing of reggae from Mr Williams' transistor radio, which was, as usual, elsewhere. Mr Williams, the porter had a trolley and a tranny with which he perambulated the hospital corridors distributing mail and essential medical supplies in time to Bob Marley and Desmond Decker. A little further down the corridor there was an open door from which at mealtimes emanated the sounds of animated conversation and the pleasant aroma of home-cooked food. A sign on the door announced, 'Doctors' Dining Room'. Inside was one large table which could comfortably sit ten people. These were the 2 or occasionally 3 consultants present that day (a general surgeon, a general physician and occasionally a gynaecologist) 4 housemen (2 medical and 2 surgical), one senior house officer (medical) and a surgical and a medical registrar. The day started at breakfast which was early and where the consultants and surgical registrar, who lived out, caught up with the admissions, crises and conundrums of the previous night. This was the hub of the organisation where most of the medical consultation

15. *In those days the term meant a long thin, single-sex ward, in use since the Crimean War, with a row of beds on each side.*

happened, referrals and second opinions were discussed. Garbled accounts of heroic interventions and confessions of less heroic ones were delivered, and anxieties aired. In half an hour over a full English or just coffee and toast (which were all free) the consultants could see how their juniors were coping or not coping. This was how a busy district general hospital worked in those days – lots of face-to-face communication – not a lot of paper – hardly any management.

Already junior doctors' hours had been reformed a bit – no longer were we expected to be ever-present but there wasn't much expectation that we would ever have the energy to leave the building on our nights off, thus wives were generally welcome, indeed they might even get a wake-up cup of coffee or tea from the doctor's maid (yes that's right) when she roused the spouse half an hour before breakfast.

Angus would stride out, his long white coat flapping with his swinging gait, pockets bulging with essential little books (the BNF, [16] the Paediatric Vade Mecum[17] and a notebook inscribed with a hundred things he must not forget and phone numbers he might need), bleep, pens, pen torch, bulky ophthalmoscope, otoscope attachments and patella hammer – also pipe, tobacco and large box of matches!

I, meanwhile, being in my final clinical year, would be off to various clinical attachments – public health in the gigantic building site that was Milton Keynes where planners for the first time were creating medical services *before* moving the patients in. Enthusiastic innovators preached *Community Chiropody* to groups of wide-eyed students without the complication of actual patients with sore feet (patients seemed destined always to be thin on the ground during my medical education). Meanwhile my husband was seeing more patients than anyone could reasonably wish for.

I went to the new spinal injuries unit at Stoke Mandeville Hospital after which I finally sold my motor bike, only a Honda 50 and very cold – I never did have the right kit. Anyway, I had never felt the same way about it after laying it down on a wet and slippery zebra crossing on Barnet Hill when a silly policewoman had stepped off the kerb in front of me without warning. The spinal ward was bulging with young men who had done something similar, only on bigger bikes and at greater

16. BNF British National Formulary – little encyclopaedia of therapeutics
17. Useful little handbook for the management of sick children

speed or just without my luck. In the long run, that policewoman who probably sensed my unsteadiness and stepped out on purpose, may have saved me from life in a wheelchair. There were girls on the ward at Stoke Mandeville too, most of whom had fallen off horses. All were lively risk-taking youngsters, optimists by nature, which was just as well as they joked about impotence and learned tricks to empty their own bladders.

I also did community paediatrics which was about all the paediatrics I got. I had a chance to hold a baby (other than just a new-born one) to find out that it had milestones – stations of the cross on its path to adulthood. These would resonate with me in later years. Two months: looks at you squarely in the eye. Four months: realises life is a laugh – wants you to play peep-bo all the time. Ten months: falls off bed. Twelve months: pulls self to standing, walks around furniture, helps self to Granny's sherry. Two years: can climb out of cot or supermarket trolley, still can't fly. Three years: enjoys rough and tumble with adults, breaks arm, social services involved. Three and a half: starts saying 'What the f***?' when confronted with a novel situation (this often follows an afternoon alone with father, grandfather or a great aunt).

Not all babies evolve in the same way, a fact bought home to me on a visit to a secret place. In the early 1970s there were still large Victorian buildings in isolated locations that hid something that, if not considered shameful by this time, was certainly shocking. I visited one of these asylums (in the true sense – places of safety) for children with various types of developmental delay or failure. This was a place of absurd human diversity. There were giant children with tiny heads who suffered from microcephaly – their bodies had long ago gone through puberty, but they functioned like handicapped toddlers. Many were blind, some deaf and blind. Others had genetic disorders rare today giving them characteristic appearances and behaviour. There were two brothers with Cockayne Syndrome – gross growth and mental retardation and premature ageing – children like little old men. Curled up in a corner, a little boy with autism studied the repetitive movement of his own hand oblivious to the hubbub that surrounded him and a child with Cri du Chat Syndrome called repeatedly like an exotic bird at the zoo.

These children, who until only recently had been categorised as various types of idiot or (less severely affected) imbeciles, were only now starting to excite the attention of the medical profession thanks to the work of a few dedicated doctors and nurses pioneering research into mental handicap, de-stigmatisation, training for sufferers and for the profession. Community care and special schools were starting to appear, and medical students would in future receive more training in the subject than just a glimpse – 'little more than a parade of rare pathological curiosities.' [18]

It was a bizarre, chaotic place and although probably not representative of the whole, this one, at least, seemed a happy place. Teenagers with Down's Syndrome were the elite class, the monitors, the voluntary carers for those who were infinitely more disabled. Big children lay on mattresses on the floor with dummies, one blind boy, I was warned when I showed an interest, would frequently pull his eye from its socket so that it lay on his cheek wobbling on its pedicle, a trick reinforced by the screams it provoked in visitors.

These were different times – many babies in the previous 20 years had been born without much antenatal care, without screening of mothers for infections like syphilis, toxoplasmosis and cytomegalovirus. Rubella had been common (no vaccination in those days). There had been little ultrasound scanning in pregnancy, hardly any outside the centres. Termination of pregnancy was not an option for a mother expecting a severely handicapped child, even if they had known – ignorance was bliss. Congenital spinal abnormalities were more common and virtually untreatable and often not suspected until a larger than normal head obstructed labour when it might be x-rayed then crudely decompressed resulting in the death of the foetus and a vaginal delivery, allowing the mother to perhaps deliver a normal baby, vaginally, next time. Sometimes a baby with hydrocephaly surprised the obstetrician at a caesarean section performed because the labour was not progressing normally. That baby may have been 'left in a chilly side room' but did not always die. Children with gross abnormalities were often abandoned by their parents – a natural reaction – an evolutionary advantage – despite civilisation – it is in our DNA. One such child lay, bedridden, unable to move her enormous heavy head,

18. *Holt K.S. and Huntley R.M. (1973) Mental Subnormality: medical training in the United Kingdom B J Med Ed 7, 197-202.*

like some sinister football mascot but tended lovingly by other young patients with less catastrophic mental and physical disability – a large, living doll. One of the carers, who had Turner's Syndrome[19], was called Lily, She was so competent at the day-to-day nursing tasks needed by this now ten-year-old child with hydrocephaly that, though well above the upper age limit of this hospital (perhaps in her late twenties though looking much, much older), she was allowed to stay on and cared selflessly for this monstrous child She turned her patient's huge head from side to side to prevent pressure sores. Lily took me through the things she did daily for her charge, very efficiently and professionally. Then she showed me back to the sunny day-room where other residents were serving afternoon tea with sandwiches and cakes that they had made and were helping to feed other residents.

This inspirational unit, supervised by a doctor who himself suffered from achondroplasia[20], challenged all our preconceptions. It was an all-age, multiracial, multicultural community of outcasts of all shapes and sizes but, thanks to the amazing staff, even the most unpromising lives seemed to have a place – a purpose.

Less inspiring was my attachment in psychiatry. This was divided into three parts. The first of these was delivered in out-patient sessions at a Hospital in Hampstead with the Freudian lady psychiatrist (FLP) who had run the student health service for many years (you have met her before). Her registrar would interview a patient at length, filmed in some primitive way (the filming) and viewed by the students in another room and then discussed with the FLP. It didn't seem as if the FLP actually saw any patients herself – there may have been good reasons for this. It was summer, it was hot, we were in a darkened room and the registrar was very thorough, in short it was very boring. I was never good at being bored (which fortunately in medicine didn't happen very often).

The very first patient was an elderly and frail, cockney lady who had been re-housed in a high-rise council flat with amazing views but dodgy lifts. Since moving she had become depressed. She had become socially isolated and felt that the loss of street life was in no

19. *Absence of one X chromosome associated with relatively mild developmental delay.*
20. *Dr, Sir William Geoffrey Shakespeare.*

way compensated for by her view which, when all said and done, was mainly of the power station and factories around the River Lea. The registrar, who knew his boss, knew to probe farther. 'Factories?' he asked. 'With chimneys?'

'Oh yes,' said the lady pleased with the registrar's sudden interest. 'Great, huge, factory chimneys, belching smoke, and the fat old cooling towers spewing steam – people say the clouds they make are pretty – I'd rather see trees!'

The FLP stopped the film and rewound it, I woke up. 'Ejaculating steam!' said the FLP, 'Erect penises! This poor woman, probably a victim all her life of the sexual exploitation of her generation ends her day with nothing to look at but the erect penises of her subjugation!'

I laughed, I laughed loudly, explosively I thought it was a joke. Oh no, everyone turned their attention on me.

'And what pray is making Miss Grant hysterical... Don't be embarrassed My Dear...' she said with venom.

'I'm sorry, I'm not embarrassed,' I said. 'That poor lady seems to me to have quite enough to make her depressed, not being able to get to the shops or see her friends and family without having to worry about phallic symbols. I'm sorry... I just thought it was a strange thing for you to say...' I was on the back foot, it was not going down well (the FLP was swelling with rage) but I continued, weakly. 'Anyway, I don't think a nice old lady like her whose got ten grandchildren and lived through two wars... By and large, with respect, would necessarily think that way.'

'OUT!' said the Freudian lady, 'Get out of my clinic!'

I did and that was an end to that third of my psychiatry course.

Fortunately, there were other psychiatrists, often speaking with East European accents, who tempered their beliefs with more common sense. Neurosis happened and was treated in Hampstead (that is where it was needed perhaps) but now out of reach for me. Psychosis ('proper' mental illness) still resided in its spiritual home which was Colney Hatch of 'You'll drive me to Coney Atch!' Despite name changes 'Colney Hatch' had long been the cockney synonym for insanity. It was remembered as the Victorian Lunatic Asylum. Now re-named Friern Hospital, it could not outlive its reputation. Not like the Maudsley Hospital (where Granny had been leucotomised) whence all the modern and more enlightened psychiatrists that you came across in London seemed to emanate (the post-graduate hub of the city's psychiatric training – home of the Institute of Psychiatry).

Of course, 'enlightened practice' in medicine often only means not practiced for long enough to know what the drawbacks are! This was the time when the enlightened were calling for the closure of hospitals like Friern with its third of a mile corridor and vast, yawning dayrooms where 'ward rounds' were held. The patient, summoned from the ward, was invited to sit in a circle with perhaps 12 students, the Professor and a registrar. After some words of introduction from the registrar the patient was asked how they fared, and all attention would focus upon them – when they hesitated the silence was savoured. Students might be asked to proffer their thoughts which often produced even more delicious pregnant pauses (the life blood of psychiatry) and opportunity for the professor to demonstrate his wise and serene forbearance.

At that time, it seemed to me, that there was a lot of muddled thinking in psychiatry which, after all, was a mixture of organic brain disease (nature – chemical abnormalities, tumours, infections, degeneration) and bitter experience (nurture – or lack of it, substance abuse and therapeutics). Superimpose on that the infinite variety of the human personality and cultures and you are faced with behaviour. Looking at the end product, the behaviour – analysing the garbled words didn't seem a very practical or scientific way of going about things.

We students visited the art therapy unit to be amazed by the work done by one patient—in another World he would have been hailed as an artist. He had lived in the hospital for many years and painted crowded canvases of naked men engaged in amorous acts – they were beautiful and reminded me of the ceiling of the Sistine Chapel except that they were on the level – not floating which would have made sex difficult and they definitely were not draped. Remember, most of his life homosexuality had been illegal and even if they had been heterosexual such unabashed representations would have doubtless landed him in jail. So, he had remained in the sanctuary of Friern Hospital painting his fantasies.

Friern Hospital was not perfect, it was dilapidated, the long-stay wards had some patients who had been there for decades and their reason for remaining was often stated as simply 'institutionalisation'[21] and patients were not infrequently spotted fornicating in the bushes of the extensive grounds – a haven for all sorts of wildlife. The interface between the patient and doctors that the students witnessed sometimes seemed combative in a strange passive way. My friend Ruth found it so troubling that she never did complete her psychiatry course – Ruth was both perceptive and empathic (a great fan of Leonard Cohen!)

Time would tell that places like Friern Hospital, despite their shortcomings, had been a sanctuary offering asylum and safety to the vulnerable and that was infinitely preferable to what followed for many inmates who were rushed into the 'community' to ultimately find themselves unsupported and living on the streets or in prison. I wondered who it was that decided that 'having a place of your own' should be the ultimate goal for the vulnerable or that living alone was good for anyone?

In the grounds of Friern was a special new unit for anorexia nervosa, which was definitely a recent, predominantly post-war phenomenon.

'I just can't stand it – it is really difficult!' I tried to explain to Mum. 'I'm supposed to get to know this patient but it's like she's not in. I can't seem to make contact with her.'

'You mean she goes out?'

'No! She's physically there but she hardly sees me. She is completely out of it.'

'Is that because of the medicine they give her?'

'No, it's the illness.'

'So they really are ill?'

'Desperately, some of them, it's really tragic, Mum – one or two have actually starved to death. They are so focused on losing weight that they don't see themselves as others do. And they ruminate all the time about food.'

'Well, you would if you were starving!'

'Yes, but not about one radish – I mean, not carefully calculating how many times you have to walk around the unit to offset a single radish! That is the level of it – there is a constant mental battle between

21. Unequipped to survive outside a given institution.

127

wanting to eat and wanting not to, or having to work it off or get away to vomit. The obsession drives everything else out of their heads (they think that may be part of it – expunging everything else from their heads – bad things – shame, sexual abuse, self-loathing, bullying, that sort of thing.'

'Oh dear, poor things.'

'We're all about the same age and they want us to interact but when I try to have a chat (you mustn't breathe a word of this to anyone Mum – *medical confidentiality*) ...' Mum nods. '...You can tell that she isn't really listening, and she misses everything that is going on around her – I asked her if she had watched the royal wedding[22] at the weekend and, would you believe it, she didn't know what I was talking about! She is so busy in her head calculating how many calories she is burning or when she can get away to do some more exercise. I suppose you are right... It is driven all the time because she is so hungry, but it is robbing her of her personality – I think that's why I find it so difficult – she's like a zombie.'

'Shall I make you a fruit cake to take in?'

'No, it would be wasted – but you can make one for us! Some of them have been there for months, they have their weight monitored and get rewards for reaching their target weight each week and get privileges if they do. Like being allowed to go out to the post box.'

'Doesn't that make them even more focused on their weight?'

'It probably does but the staff have to have some objective measure of their progress and warning if they are going down. The girl I'm paired with, I can't tell you her name, is pitifully thin but she pinches at her skin and moans that she is obscenely obese – sometimes I want to shake her – chase her round the grounds – make her see that there is a big wide world out there!'

'Do you remember me telling you when you were bored once – you were about sixteen – that you only get out of life what you are prepared to put in?

'Yes Mum...'

'That's when you went and volunteered at the hospital. Perhaps she

22. *Princess Anne and Captain Mark Phillips*

could do some Voluntary Service – I don't think we had anorexia in the war!' said Mum as she peeled the last potato and popped it in the pot.

In the evenings, if it was a night off for Angus, we would return to our rooms in South Hampstead where I would cook supper during which Angus often fell asleep. When he was on call in the evening I went to Cricklewood Memorial and might cook something for the on-call team. Living with those on-call, sitting in the mess in the evenings chatting to them as they came and went was a good way of absorbing a lot of medicine. If they had a big case to do at night, I might even scrub up to assist in theatre. It was during one such episode, when Angus had been sent to the ward to prep the next case and I was helping the surgeon to close up, that Angus's boss asked me if I would like to be his houseman when the time came – I said I would – there was nothing anonymous about selection in those days.

On days without clinical attachments of my own I would sit at the desk in Angus's room overlooking the front of the hospital, the frosted lower panes obscuring all but the waving tops of the trees, listening to the wind and studying for my finals.

After six months, Angus moved on to do his house physician's job at another repurposed Victorian asylum for the sick in Bow, East London (an area long since razed to the ground and redeveloped, and not before time). The hospital was a sinister, soot stained, monolith that teetered, seemingly on the verge of collapse, inches from the railway lines that carried the underground trains of the Hammersmith, Circle and District Lines to and from the centre of the city. Trains hurtled past every twenty seconds rattling the old building to its core. There was no escape – Angus's dingy, north facing room gave directly onto the railway, the windows giving a permanently sepia view of the tenements opposite and rattling with the approach of the next train. At night, so rough was the area, guard dogs were released into the strip of gravelled ground between building and high iron railings. I liked dogs but these were huge, skinny, snarling timber wolves, delivered at dusk, muzzled and chained, and released with a flourish by tattooed men. I did not visit often, this was the Bow of the Kray brothers and made Cricklewood, Kilburn, Willesden and Acton seem like the Garden of Eden.

With Angus working or asleep at home there was nothing to distract me – I punctuated my disappointingly patient-free senior medicine course with student locums. I worked as a house officer at the Renal Unit where I had real *life-and-death* motivation to find out the best answers to the endless questions that arose in a day. I had already passed the examinations of both royal colleges[23] so, technically was 'qualified' so even got paid for being in this unique learning situation. You could take the various exams in the final year getting the MRCS[24] and the LRCP[24], these could be taken separately and repeated any number of times – it was an exercise in not putting your eggs in one basket. It tended to be what London students did – an insurance policy against missing or failing your university finals. If you did get the flu or have a nervous breakdown in finals week there was then nothing to stop you starting your house jobs without your London University degree[26]. It took the pressure off.

Now you would think that passing finals would be a mighty cause for celebration but by that stage everyone was so keen to get on with the next stage of life that it often passed almost un-noticed. People were moving to new areas to take up house jobs elsewhere, they were getting married, having babies or going abroad for long furloughs. Angus and I bought a house.

23. *The Royal College of Surgeons and the Royal College of Physicians*
24. *Member of the Royal College of Surgeons*
25. *Licentiate of the Royal College of Physicians*
26. *MBBS (hons)*

Chapter 21.

North Finchley and Cricklewood

Our new house was about 60 yards from the North Circular Rd in North London, a twenty minute drive from my parents' and about the same, traffic permitting from Cricklewood Memorial where, you might remember, I had arranged to work. Thirty-five minutes the other way took Angus into the industrial wasteland of the Thames estuary in Essex to his new job in A&E.[27]

Angus was now set firmly on the path of surgery and I approved. William Osler (1849 - 1919), one of the fathers of modern medicine recognised that a surgeon required: [28] 'Coolness and presence of mind under all circumstances, calmness amid storm, clearness of judgment in moments of grave peril, immobility, impassiveness.' This was Angus all over. Osler also advised 'a certain measure of insensibility' as 'not only an advantage, but a positive necessity in the exercise of a calm judgement, and in carrying out delicate operations.' This I had also worked out and it was a game saver. Angus could concentrate to the exclusion of all else – when focused, which he usually was, he lost all consciousness of the world around him, a tiny bit of his brain maintained his posture – but don't be deceived – he was not there – he was deep in a sick man's abdomen or under the bonnet of his car. This could have been irritating to live with, but I thought it was a great gift, which of course it is. I knew he was going to be a very good surgeon.

A lot of our waking hours at home (there were not many) were spent in the steam and condensation of our little bathroom with its half-glassed door and stained-glass window. Angus, exhausted from work, would lie in the bath, marinating, and I sat on the floor with a concise handbook of operative surgery open on my knee. Each operation was described, as in a recipe book with numbered steps. Angus was consigning them to memory, breathing in the information cunningly nebulised in the steam and I was testing him – after a year I had adsorbed so much of the fall-out that I could also recite most

27. *Accident and Emergency*
28. *Aequanimitas by William Osler, P Blakiston's son & co 1925*

operations like the fiddly way to remove a parotid tumour, laying open the face and neck with flaps, avoiding all the important structures in a 'commando' operation, avoiding the facial nerve – it was the last operation in the book and quite specialised. Years later I might be quietly writing up my notes in an A&E office or in the corner of some ward or the ante-room of an operating theatre when my ears would interrupt my thoughts with a snatch of conversation or teaching of a surgical colleague recounting some procedure. If he omitted a stage, I would pipe up a reminder. It was only a reflex but disconcerting for the colleague – like a priest talking confidentially to the Dean in Latin and having his grammar corrected by the church cleaner on her knees scrubbing the floor.

Not surprisingly Angus passed both parts of his FRCS on the first attempt and at the earliest possible opportunity.

Unlike most aspiring surgeons he was avoiding the ivory towers in favour of operative experience – not for him the easy life of a teaching hospital – he wanted operative experience, and lots of it, so he went where the patients were. Thus, for many years he worked very hard and was filling up his surgical logbook with tens of some operations and hundreds of others. After the mandatory six months of A&E he worked at a large new district general hospital in Hertfordshire under a respected consultant who had a passion for operating and teaching – Angus had found a soul mate.

Bearing in mind the nepotism that existed within the profession at that time with powerful figures within the teaching hospitals and royal colleges boasting that they looked after their own and were heavily represented on appointment committees – burying himself in the periphery was not necessarily a very sound strategy though it suited someone who could not tolerate bullshit. At a time when contemporaries were talking a good cholecystectomy[29] and fighting each other to assist their boss doing one, Angus had done three supervised and fifty-six on his own[30]. Keeping a logbook of his surgery would turn out to be a masterstroke when it came to job interviews in the future – there was to be no arguing with his experience.

29. *Removal of gall bladder*
30. *Figures uncorroborated but you get my drift.*

Chapter 22.

Another World

Although by now a married woman and a rate payer I looked much younger than my twenty-four years when I donned my long white coat (much too long) and stepped onto the wards of Cricklewood Memorial. These were the days of a dress code for professional women – not only did I pound the miles of corridor throughout the day and most of the night but did so in a short skirt and high heeled shoes – this convention, like the binding of girls' feet in China finally died out in the second half of the twentieth century. Some said it existed as an ornamentation of these handmaidens – or possibly a sign of their high station and professionalism. The truth, in China at least, was that it stopped young women from getting frisky and avoiding the boring, sedentary piece work that was their lot. Whatever the reason, a whole generation of female medical practitioners was crippled by this cruel custom. A lady house officer was certainly never expected to be sedentary but there was to be no slobbing about in surgical scrubs and trainers (not even at night) as there might be today, with a stethoscope draped lightly around the shoulders. These were the days of heavy, steel, hinged stethoscopes with rubber tubes and ceramic earpieces – mine clung to my neck with its little arms, like a baby animal, its tail waving as I walked, or curled up asleep in one of my capacious pockets.

My opposite number, the other houseman (nothing was gender neutral) was Phil. He was tall and thin with long untidy hair and the slightly toxic air of someone driven by adrenaline – fine tremor, excessive perspiration, boundless good humour and a huge appetite (he never ate less than two meals at any one sitting). He was hard working, always willing and competent but self-effacing (largely based on the fact that he had extraordinarily bad luck). All the difficult, scary cases arrived on his take.

God seemed determined to stretch Phil to the very limit – like the time the policeman had a pneumothorax: *'When I put the chest drain in, he collapsed (no one told me to attach the underwater seal first or put my thumb over the end) – I thought – that's it! I've killed a policeman!'*

The death penalty for murdering a police officer had actually been abolished four years earlier but Phil had had his head down at the time.

Phil or I manned the surgical take at night with only a registrar of dubious ability on the end of an unreliable telephone. When things got really tough, we called each other, if still around, if not then we called the boss (bypassing the middleman). The bosses came quickly – they knew how precarious was the cover.

I was learning fast from my own experience and as much again from listening to Phil's hair-raising accounts of the night before as he tucked into his second breakfast: '... *Stabbed in the neck, blood everywhere...* *When you take the pressure dressing off you have to have them head* *down, otherwise they suck air into their jugular vein and die! Thank* *God Sister had seen one before – when I arrived, she'd already got him on* *the tipping table... I thought she'd gone mad.'*

*

For six months we two young people blundered from one potential disaster to the next. This was a violent area and for some strange reason (probably financial) between the hours of 6pm and midnight on weekend nights there were only two doctors on duty for the whole hospital, the surgical and the medical houseman. The busy A&E was manned by the surgical houseman (the most junior doctor in the place). The cases that confronted us in this, our very first substantive post, staggered into the department often leaving a trail of blood and leading a flotilla of inebriated and over-excited friends and relatives.

But we were not alone: there was Sister O'Malley, 4ft 2ins, from Limerick, she could emasculate an aggressive psychopath with one lash of her tongue, and she moved so fast and efficiently that a huge stroppy drunk became mesmerised by her, as if a fly was buzzing around his head – he became dizzy and sank, compliant onto the nearest trolley whence Sister, helped by the one student nurse, would remove his trousers and do his observations. So small but powerful was she that warring factions were soon segregated and given useful tasks to complete – filling in forms for each other, telephoning relatives and helping push friends round to x-ray. Confidence, I learned, was everything.

Under Sister O'Malley's quick, watchful guiding eye, Phil and I (on alternate weekends) resuscitated, disarmed, intubated, ventilated, catheterised, lanced, sutured and washed out the stomachs of the citizens of Cricklewood, Kilburn, Acton and Willesden. We gave them bad news and good news, cups of tea and arranged for them to be sectioned under the mental health act. We plastered their un-displaced fractures and replaced their dislocated shoulders. Neither of us was ever sued!

One of the hazards of working at this hospital was the risk of bubonic plague. It was a theoretical hazard, extrapolated from the high incidence of flea bites among the emergency staff. When the crash bleep[31] went off the quickest route from one ward to the next was out though the French windows at the end of one ward and in through the French windows of the ward with the emergency – this added to the general impression for patients of being in a French farce. The worried looking student nurse (there was only ever one) would rapidly pull the curtains round a bed and make haste to the sister's office to telephone, a moment later the windows at the end of the ward would burst open and assorted, white coated youngsters would tumble in and run up the ward slapping their legs and occasionally pausing to pull up a trouser leg. If the floor was being mopped at least one would skid and fall spewing medical detritus and expletives.

The thing was that the grounds around the hospital were populated by many feral cats and rats attracted by the food left by a dear old lady who lived nearby and liked cats. However, the dominant species was undoubtedly *Siphonaptera*, the cat flea, who dropped their eggs carelessly into the grass where they hatched into little orphan fleas. These were hungry and eager to be adopted by any passing mammal – if nothing more feline was available, a lady houseman's lightly stockinged leg was ideal but even the woolly sock of her male colleague was comforting.

One day, when one of the feral cats was found blooded and injured, dragging itself toward the door of A&E, the junior staff now bristling with confidence and new clinical skill switched instantly into heroic mode. The creature looked tabby with tyre marks, in fact it was white except for one tortoiseshell ear (the left) and a ginger tip to its tail, it was examined, movement was painful, a trolley was commandeered,

31. *The emergency call for the cardiac arrest team.*

135

Pussy was wheeled to x-ray where the radiographer was drawn into the drama. Miss P. Cat (the name on the x-ray) had sustained compound multiple fractures of her femur, tibia and fibula and her pelvis didn't look too chipper (none of us was very sure what it should look like). Pride comes before a fall and we all knew that this was the one case that was way beyond our ability, even pooling our knowledge and possibly calling in an orthopaedic colleague – the situation was hopeless. (Arranging an ambulance to 'blue light' Pussy to the Royal Vet College, we agreed, was probably a bridge too far). So, sadly we requisitioned an ampule of heroin from the crash trolley and injected the little cat with all of it. We laid her lovingly under the rhododendron bush by the casualty entrance and withdrew.

As we emerged from the bushes, we encountered the night porter returning to his post after a temporary absence – he had had a good night and presented us with two large brown trout.

Next day the cat had gone, we nodded knowingly to each other – a predator, or possibly God, had intervened.

That is not the end of the story. Some weeks later, the weather was hot, the surgical ward-round had progressed to the gigantic gentleman with a pituitary tumour who rejoiced in the name of Horse (for very good reasons to which I could attest although the very thought of it made me squeamish). His tumour had been dealt with in the neurosurgical unit of a teaching hospital from which, so interesting was his case, he thought he would never escape. Now he needed a hernia repair but that is immaterial to the tale. Sir Bors Helvig, the consultant surgeon, was red faced and sweating in his heavy three-piece, grey suit, he mopped his brow with a handkerchief, no nurse having stepped forward to do it for him. 'Op'n the window, Darlin' he said – that was the way he addressed lady doctors, men he grunted their approximate surname, but he was enough of a gentleman to know that that was no way to address a lady. I clicked professionally to the French window and opened it. As I did so a small white cat, with one tortoiseshell ear, the left, and a ginger tip to its tail, strutted in. The cat threw a gracious glance at the white coated doorman and proceeded up the centre of the ward, tail in the air and without so much as a limp, in fact she moved quite agilely when pursued by a large surgical sister yelling something unintelligible (to all but the cat).

This was several years before the miracle of Barry Sheen's[32] broken leg but taught the members of the junior staff that however much they think they know – sometimes things just get better by themselves!

*

Cats were not the only hazard. There was predation of other types, at least that is how it seemed to me who still had a great deal to learn about human sexuality. I had grasped the notion of sexual attraction between peers, not members of the aristocracy but people like me and Angus, equals, who fell in love and lived happily ever after. It was to be a long time before I understood that sexual attraction could pop up in all sorts of unlikely settings and between all sorts of seemingly disparate people.

Sister Jameson worked nights, she was senior with greying hair, worn in a tight bun, she was quite slim and very pleasant. Had I given it any thought I might have conceded that Sister Jameson was still of a childbearing age, but I had not. She wore the navy-blue rank of authority, the silver buckle of professionalism. 'But x-ray is closed!' I said to Pranal, the switchboard operator, 'What is Night Sister doing there? I'm trying to find Dr Norton, his bleep isn't working and he's not in his room, I thought she might know where he is – his wife is in the mess waiting for him – she's brought in his birthday cake.'

'Woops!' said Pranal, 'I'll tell them – mums the word.'

'What? Oh, he's gone...' I put down the mess receiver and turned to the wife, sitting nursing a cake tin and a pile of cards in a battered armchair in the little room above the doctor's dining room. 'Someone must have collapsed in X-ray – he'll be along in a minute. How are the children?'

Only after I had said this did I realise how well I had covered, innocence being the best cloak for deceit.

Minutes later Nick Norton arrived, red faced and flustered, 'You should phone first if you are coming over,' he said to his wife ungraciously.

'I did! I spoke to someone called Phil. He said if there was cake, I should come immediately!'

32. Barry Sheen, World Champion and severely smashed up motor cyclist whose orthopaedic rebuilding became legendary.

'Happy Birthday, Nick!' I said as Phil was heard coming up the stairs three at a time, 'shall I get plates?'

*

Pranal, the switchboard operator was at the heart of the hospital – he was the whole reason it worked. He sat in a cell at the centre of everything like a queen bee, connected and invisibly, imperceptibly directing – he seemed to know everything. He was young, the same age as the housemen (he had the same birthday as me). He was clever and inquisitive – had life not dealt him such a physical blow (paraplegia and Crohn's disease which had withered his legs and chained him to a wheelchair which in turn was chained to the adjacent lavatory) he would certainly have been a captain of industry, an underworld don or, at the very least, a successful comedian and compere of the Royal Variety Performance. Instead, he sat in a darkened room surrounded by primitive electrical equipment and switchboard apparatus from whence he monitored and controlled everything in an almost sinister Orwellian way. Born thirty years later, even with his disabilities, he would have made a fortune playing computer games or running a hedge fund. As it was, he ran a small district general hospital by stealth. Monitoring all the telephonic traffic, he knew everything that went on from the private enterprise schemes running in the kitchen, the ETA[33] of the various consultants and their sexual proclivities, the state of health of Night Sister's mother-in-law and Mrs Patel's haemoglobin. At all times, he knew (without any sort of satnav) the exact location of every member of staff by plotting their every movement in his head and adjusted it using his intimate knowledge of their personal habits. He knew which patient was sick and which wasn't and where their relatives were. When there was a crash call and the terrified new houseman had garbled the message, Pranal knew exactly where to send the team. He knew the rotas of adjacent hospitals and the reputation of the various specialists. 'Put me through to the Central Middlesex Pran, we've got some urgent burr holes[34] need blue lighting.'

33. *Estimated Time of Arrival*
34. *Burr holes: surgical intervention to reduce inter-cranial pressure and reduce dangerously increased pressure within the skull – done with a sort of Black & Decker and not usually by the houseman.*

'I wouldn't recommend that tonight – Mr Pancceta is on take – I'll put you through to the Royal and Ancient – the ambulance is on its way and I've asked for a police escort.'

That was how it went but always subtle. Not like Frank Merriweather who manned the switchboard in Pranal's absence and was forty years older – he did his best but often gave himself away. My mother had phoned me one day at work to confirm that Angus and I were expected for supper, when asked if she would like us to bring anything, she had mentioned that it didn't matter but she could do with some frozen peas. Later that day just before I left the hospital I called in to the switchboard to say I was leaving the building, 'I'm off now Frank, where's the best place round here to buy some flowers?'

'Maples on Cricklewood Broadway, just passed the station, you can park round the corner.'

'Thanks Frank! Bye!'

'Bye-bye Doc. Don't forget the frozen peas!'

*

These were the days before political correctness, before confidentiality, before protocols and procedures. 'See one, do one, teach one' was the mantra for learning to practice medicine, so you had to pay attention when you saw something done (like a catheter insertion or the aspiration of a breast cyst or the insertion of a central line or a chest drain) because the next time you would quite possibly be on your own and soon after that you would be telling someone else how to do it.

One evening I was struggling to catheterise an old gentleman on the ward, I had had several attempts, the bed was littered with the now unsterile wreckage of my previous attempts and the organ in question was cowering under the weight of dressing towels. The man's bladder already fit to burst was screaming with the extra fluid that was dripping into his arm from the drip that I had managed to insert into a vein. He was becoming more and more distressed and with every groan my hands sweated more and my clumsiness and agitation increased.

As fate would have it, Sir Bors suddenly and unexpectedly appeared at the end of the bed, 'Alright Darlin? Any problems?'

'Well only this catheter... I can't seem to get it past the... I've tried two smaller ones but...'

'Oh dear, let me...' He was pushing up the sleeve of his jacket.

'Wouldn't you like to scrub up, Sir?' I asked weakly.

'No! It's all in the tissues!' he trumpeted. 'If you don't traumatise the tissues, they won't get infected… These are all far too small.'

'What size would you like?'

'This one!' he said pulling a large catheter from his jacket pocket, 'Always carry one, (knew a chap once who used to keep one in the lining of his bowler hat) – there's no one more grateful than the man with acute retention who you can relieve without delay.' So, saying he slipped the catheter into the man's terrified penis and, sure enough, a serene smile immediately crossed the man's face as the bed filled with urine. 'Bag, Girl! Bag!'

'Woops!' I fumbled to connect the urine bag. 'I'll get some saline to fill the balloon.'

'No, no, no, hand me that syringe.' He disconnected the bag for a moment and thrust in the syringe drawing up the patient's own urine, handed me back the bag to reconnect to one arm of the catheter while he injected the urine through the other arm to inflate the balloon at its tip so that it couldn't slip out. For that instant we were a team – wow! Then he dematerialised, slipping out of the cone of light into the darkened ward as quickly as he had appeared, leaving me to clear up the evidence of my lack of experience and profligate use of resources.

*

The life of a London teaching hospital consultant was punctuated by formal events – dinners, not 'in college' as they might have been in Oxford of Cambridge, but in the banqueting halls of the capital and in one's royal college or as guests at other royal colleges or one of the City's Worshipful Companies. Maybe if the president of your college was a naval man that year, you might have a formal dinner in the splendid surroundings of the Royal Naval College in Greenwich, or the House of Lords or Lambeth Palace – it was how connections were made – all very civilised – reciprocal –what we now call networking.

To introduce those coming up in the profession and to reward them for the hours of unpaid work they did to facilitate their boss's private practice and academic pursuits and for their discretion, every six months or so, usually near the end of your appointment if you were a houseman, you would be taken as a guest to one of these dinners.

This was another insidious hoop, as your dress, table manners and social graces could be scrutinised as a potential, future colleague.

Angus and I dined at the Ritz, the Savoy and several times at the Café Royal (my particular favourite). On one occasion we dined at Greenwich. I felt particularly aptly dressed in a purple velvet gown, embroidered lavishly with gold thread with a neckline that plunged almost to my umbilicus. No bra could be found to adapt itself to this cleavage so one of the sisters taped my bosoms with expensive, very sticky and translucent tape used in the operating theatre as an occlusive dressing – she assured me that it was what film actresses used. That night was memorable for half the men, those not in dinner jackets, were in dress uniform – the scarlet of the jackets of Royal Marines bouncing off the glittering candelabras and gilded scrolls of the extravagant baroque walls to blend with the reds and gold of the swirling figures on the painted ceiling and walls. The Sistine Chapel's decoration would pale into insignificance by comparison – however, to be fair, I'd had a lot less to drink when I viewed Michelangelo's ceiling. With the copious wine, the port and the antique uniformed, gold-trimmed flunkies the atmosphere was positively Napoleonic! I should say Nelsonian, though he never styled himself an emperor!

The whole point of these dinners was not the ambrosia of privilege, nor even the euphoria of intoxication but to establish the hierarchy of the various after-dinner speakers. The quality of after-dinner speeches seemed to me to be very good, very amusing and clever – it was one of the precursors of 'stand-up' and also required a lubricated audience. I particularly enjoyed the story of the patient on a ward round who was told to take things easy, work less and enjoy himself more. He looked puzzled and asked whether sex should be considered work or pleasure. The narrator, a consultant, felt it was probably about 25% pleasure and 75% work but was not dogmatic and asked the registrar what he thought. The registrar reckoned it was about 50/50. 'Ah!' said the houseman. 'That can't be right, it must be 100% pleasure – if there was any work in it, you lot would have me doing it!'

This joke was always well received – I heard it a number of times! It had that element of truth which is the hallmark of a good gag.

The thing was – in earlier days, but even in my days as a houseman, the juniors worked very hard for little reward, but with seniority came the power to delegate and considerable rewards. As a consultant coasted towards retirement, he could take things more easily – leave more to his juniors – take advantage of his seniority – pass on his knowledge and experience without getting out of bed too many times. Since that time, with increasing equality, advancing seniority has carried less and less power and privilege and less opportunity to adapt as one ages, and we all age. It is one reason that so many doctors opt to retire early – to be honest, they simply can't do it anymore.

Chapter 23.

Murder

Sir Bors Helvig had a habit of being there when needed – fuelling my suspicion that someone other than just Pranal was taking an overview of our lives.

The police attitude to domestic violence at that time was, shall we say, fatalistic – *what will be, will be.* They had learned something about female sexuality that I would only learn later, that is that realising what a bastard she lives with, and doing something about it, has as much to do with a woman's hormones as it has to do with her partner's violent behaviour. It was strange that members of the constabulary should grasp this before the medical profession. Hormones, you see, come and go every couple of weeks so it works like this: she calls the police on one day of the month when she is pre-menstrual and not pregnant. Mother Nature is thinking about changing the stud because she is not getting pregnant so allows her to see him more clearly – she feels aggrieved by his shortcomings, if not a little aggressive herself. When they come to blows the police arrest him and bail him to appear in court later. Later coincides with another day in her cycle, say ovulation, and not wishing to waste a single egg, Mother Nature produces a surge of *oh-I-do-love-him* hormone and the woman withdraws her allegations and the police case collapses. Thus, in the interest of not wasting effort, the police were very reluctant to come between man and wife. If you look at the crime statistics of that time you will find meticulously recorded rates for bicycle theft and all the different types of burglary and different categories of sexual offence, depending on the age and gender of the victim, but murder, manslaughter and infanticide are all lumped together so who knows what was really going on – whether things have got better or worse. Undoubtedly many women were being murdered by their partners, unrecorded – not until the scale of the problem was recognised did the police and home office start to take more notice.

One night a young woman with severe facial injuries appeared mysteriously in Casualty. a dark-haired young man with grazed knuckles was hovering in the waiting room and around the door to the department, coming and going edgily, agitated and anxiously looking into the cubicles as if trying to find someone but avoiding staff, avoiding their eye contact. The young woman was evasive about her injuries, she was x-rayed and tidied up but rather than sending her home with an appointment for the facio-maxillary department at another hospital later in the week, she was admitted to the ward. No-one who spoke to her was in any doubt that she had taken a severe beating and was frightened, she did not want to talk to the police but as was very often the case, two officers were in the sister's office drinking tea. One, picking up on the general concern for this girl, roused himself, went out into the corridor drawing himself up to his full height, brushing back his hair and putting on his helmet. Beyond him, out in the waiting room, I noticed the dark-haired man scuttle out of the building. The young woman now remembered that she had tripped over the dog and hit her face on the corner of a table and refused to talk to the police officer. Next day she was collected from the ward by her husband, a dark-haired young man bearing flowers in a roughly bandaged hand (he told the sister he had sprained his wrist).

The day after that the surgical team were doing a ward round with Sir Bors, it comprised four or five young men in white coats, we had a few students at the time, Phil and me, and we had parked ourselves in a quiet backwater of the corridor system where double rubber doors opened to admit and discharge the large laundry trolleys and bins. We were disturbed by a kerfuffle in the main corridor, I poked my head around the corner to see the young woman of the day before struggling to get away from an attacker who holding her by one arm was raining blows about her head with the other. Most of the noise was coming from a tall young man in a white coat with a shock of bobbing curly brown hair and an extravagantly droopy moustache who was easily identified as Jim the house physician who was remonstrating with the young man. The assailant was ignoring him. I relayed this information back to the ward round. Now Sister Boateng entered the fray, coming out of her ward to investigate. Her arrival and the addition of her booming baritone to the barrage of disapproval distracted the young perpetrator and his victim pulled away. She ran screaming down the corridor pursued by the young man leaving Jim and Sister Boateng looking shocked.

At this moment Uri the Ukrainian theatre technician was proceeding up the corridor pushing a prostrate gynae patient on a bed that bristled with drips, oxygen cylinders and a student nurse. The fleeing girl's path was thus blocked, and she swerved past me into the loading bay, hurtling down the ramp towards the knot of surgeons at the bottom. As she ran into the group Sir Bors stepped sideways interposing himself between her and her pursuer. He stood, a mountain of a man in his three-piece grey suit, his large abdomen making a kind of statement. The young man stopped and shouted that it was his own wife he was trying to catch.

Sir Bors took one step forward. 'This,' he boomed. 'Is a hospital!' And taking another step forward he butted the man with his great waist-coated belly, the young man staggered sideways and bounced off the wall swearing then regaining his balance, bolted through the double doors and was gone.

'Sanctuary!' said Sir Bors. 'They run to this place for sanctuary... Eh, Sister? You had better sort out this young lady...' and she and Jim led the terrified girl away to await the arrival of the police.

Sir Bors gathered his thoughts. 'Now where was I? Ah yes, injured bile ducts... Sir Anthony Eden...'[35]

Two days later a police officer arrived early in the morning wanting to take a statement from Jim about the incident. 'So you are going to prosecute him after all,' said Jim.

'Oh yes, he's only gone and murdered her. Found her body on the wasteland this morning – looks as if she might have been trying to get here again, poor kid – only nineteen.'

*

During my time at Cricklewood there were more murders that cast their shadow over the little hospital – I counted six including the pleasant young man admitted in police custody with a strangulated hernia. He lay for a week or so, handcuffed to his iron bedstead next to Sister's office while his attendant constables made themselves generally

35. *Sir Anthony Eden developed a stricture of his common bile duct (much quoted) as a result of less than perfect surgery which had to be corrected in America to the great embarrassment of the British surgical establishment*

145

useful. They helped nurse the shackled man (who had also been charged with murdering his wife). They opened recalcitrant bottles and unjammed stubborn skylights, helped to serve meals and stood up and cleared their throats if a relative showed signs of becoming impatient with the system.

The malefactor meanwhile was young, handsome and polite, seemingly grateful for the care he was receiving – quite the antithesis of a brutal killer. No one asked him about his alleged crime and when he recovered enough to go back to his cell their departure left a strange absence in the ward.

On the other side of the road from the hospital, in a detached house, slept the overflow housemen – Jim, who you have just met, and the other house physician Nick. Having already survived six months in the medical profession they were judged to have attained sufficient seniority to be trusted to cross the road in the middle of the night. This is not as silly as it sounds. The houses on that side of the road were pre-war villas with large gardens backing on to the cemetery. They were generally held to be spooky and that was before what happened in the house next door.

Nobody had actually met the neighbours, a quiet, mature couple – respectable, always together: she was rotund and smiling; he was thin, stooped and silent and wore a skullcap. They returned from business, often after dark and parked their old Humber in the elliptical drive, in front of their house. They left for work early – their movements only occasionally discerned by the young medical staff in the next house because of the security lights that flashed on and off with their comings and goings – a novelty in 1974 and irritating on stormy nights when the swaying trees at the edge of the cemetery caused them to flash on and off during the night.

It was later established that the couple owned a jewellery business on the Edgeware Road. This might have explained the need for security lighting and was thought to explain their brutal murders. All this was reported to the neighbours by a series of Chinese whispers originating from young police officers fraternising with student nurses who fraternised with junior doctors who told their bosses (which added authenticity when they passed it on to other colleagues over lunch).

By the time the two murders were examined publicly in the Coroner's Court, the house staff had long gone. Whether the person or persons unknown who were responsible were ever apprehended is lost in the frenetic career entropy of the medical profession. Hearsay had it at the time that gangsters (whom I had never come across before) had shinned over the wall from the cemetery, entered the house by forcing the French windows and grill within. They held the couple hostage for several days over a long weekend while torturing them in various imaginative ways culminating in the use of some sort of vice, large enough to accommodate a human head. This, presumably an untested technique, proved ineffective for extracting the required information – thought to be the location and combination of a safe, either real or supposed. Treating someone in such a way, it turned out, can actually silence them permanently, very suddenly. Both victims were found dead several days later – there did not appear to be a safe.

Life, it seemed to me, was considerably more precarious than my parents and schoolteachers had led me to believe.

*

What makes a gentle giant turn into a patricidal murderer? This I pondered a week or two later as I plunged a large needle into the old man's abdomen in Casualty, withdrawing copious amounts of blood confirming my worst fears – this was the sort of thing one did before one had scans. The gentle giant in question who had hit his dad in the stomach with a shovel was now standing anxiously over me as I proceeded. The police had been called and were just arriving but it had not crossed anyone's mind that the now repentant son represented any sort of danger. He was just getting in the way as were the police now, as I tried to run some O-negative blood[36] into the drip as fast as I could and the porter manoeuvred the trolley out of the tiny cubicle toward the operating theatre. The surgeon had already arrived, he had taken a brief look at the patient who was lapsing into unconsciousness. 'There is no anaesthetist yet, Sir!' I said.

'Then we shall have to start without him! Chop-chop, Miss Grant! Let's get a wriggle on!' said Mr Muir as he sped off to the theatre to get out of his dinner jacket before the blood bath began.

36. *This blood type, known as 'universal donor' blood was given in emergencies when there was insufficient time to cross match a more suitable transfusion.*

Removing the greater part of an old man's liver (most of which had to be scooped out into a bucket) with his abdomen full of blood, his blood pressure unrecordable, with a skeleton staff in the middle of the night gave a very poor prognosis. Even when the surgical registrar arrived to help and the medical SHO joined in, helping to re-transfuse blood from the suction bottle the way he had learned in Sri Lanka during the troubles – stopping the bleeding was almost impossible. But the hospital's one pathologist, Dr Celia Crabbage, a large, elderly and very cantankerous woman was prised from her bed and reluctantly came in (which she had not done for many years) to sort out the demand for blood and the clotting problems inherent in such huge transfusions. As mentioned before this was the era when everyone could turn their hand to everything and, although Dr Crabbage would never forgive me for calling her in, her intervention seemed effective – the stream of blood became a trickle that became an ooze which was packed, and the anaesthetist eventually announced that he had got a blood pressure.

As we wheeled the old gent out of the theatre and to the ward, there was a police officer waiting. He had been there half the night, for it was now daylight and the smell of bacon was wafting down the corridor. 'GBH then Doc? Not murder,' he said, rather disappointed.

I learned a lot from that experience: primarily that rescuing elderly, unhealthy folk from the jaws of death was one thing but it was just the beginning – keeping them alive was another matter altogether. You had to treat their infections, their renal failure, their D.T.s [37] and/or the myocardial infarction that would carry them off a few days later. This old boy died suddenly of a massive heart attack later in the week, after he had made peace with his son but before he could thwart the constabulary's attempts to prosecute the son for his grievous bodily harm. The greater crime, however, was undoubtedly getting Dr Celia Crabbage out of her bed.

The court case raised a number of points, which went some way to answering my original question – firstly the victim had been roaring drunk at the time having spent the day drinking homemade rum on his allotment while his wife harvested broad beans and his son, a big

37. *Delirium tremens – hallucinations (the pink elephants), low blood sugar and fits associated with the sudden withdrawal of alcohol in a chronic alcoholic.*

148

lad who was said to be slow, was digging the area from which they had recently removed the pea plants. Her innocent remark about the number of blackflies on the beans and the disappointing crop was perceived as criticism and her husband had flown into a rage, slapping his wife about the head, causing her to fall, then kicking her as she lay on the ground. This was when the son stepped forward and, with the shovel that was in his hand, took a swing at his father – more of a shove really – catching him a single blow on his not inconsiderable belly. Mr Muir gave evidence as to the parlous, enlarged and fragile state of his chronically rum soaked liver which bled into its capsule which then ruptured causing severe blood loss and his immediate collapse. The prolonged period of shock that this caused may well have damaged his heart, but so might his alcoholism, his diabetes, his hypertension and his passion for patties from the chip shop in Acton. The son was discharged without a blot on his character and from time to time thereafter a sack of carrots or bunch of beetroot would be left at the porter's lodge for Mr Muir.

And me… I learned never to pre-judge anything – there is always much more to things than you think!

Chapter 24.

Misunderstandings

When I first saw the young woman with the drawn-on eyebrows I thought .... 'I haven't seen brows like that since those two old whores in Soho...' I was learning, you see. Was it experience or prejudice? The young woman was sixteen and complained of abdominal pain and had been admitted from the gynae out-patients for urgent investigation. She had a vaginal discharge, profuse and unpleasant, testing positive for gonorrhoea, syphilis and (that new kid on the block –) chlamydia. She had a sexually transmitted hat-trick – three strikes and she was out and so early in her new career – a very old one.

That week there was a new addition to the doctor's mess, a young man on clinical attachment. A young man – tall, dark, handsome and confident (but with limited English) who had made his parents very proud by passing all his exams in his own country where he had qualified as a doctor and who now embarking on a process of induction within the National Health Service to get the required additional certification to work in the United Kingdom.

The good-looking young doctor was sent to clerk the latest surgical admissions including the young lady from the previous paragraph. As he drew the curtains around her bed (he had not understood the injunction to take a chaperone), there was only one thing that the young woman could think of to do with him. So impressed was he by the generous, discrete and loving nature of the local population that he returned immediately to the mess and boasted about it to the other young men. 'I've been here one day and already I have beautiful girlfriend.'

'That's nice, what's her name?' asked Phil

'Bethan.'

Where d'you meet her?

'On surgical ward – first bed on right.'

'Shit!' Pause, as male colleagues exchanged helpless looks, I looked up from my book and threw an encouraging glance at Phil. 'Err... Mate, there is a sort of rule in England that doctors don't have sex with their patients,' said Phil.

'Especially not if they have gonorrhoea,' I added without looking up again.

Later that day I discharged Bethan with a big box of antibiotics to take away and a follow-up appointment for out-patients. I wish I could say that a social worker then transported her to a hostel in the home-counties (a place of safety) but these were different times. What in fact happened was that she met her new boyfriend outside the ward who walked her openly up to his on-call room, nodding to colleagues on the way. The young couple did not emerge until the following morning.

The consultant to whom this young doctor was attached was quietly informed over breakfast. He held his head and quietly muttered expletives as the narrative unfurled. 'Where is he now?' asked the boss.

'Walking her to the bank, to get some money, and to the tube,' said Phil.

'He'll be back shortly, it's not far. Cultural misconceptions, Sir,' added Jim the house physician, who was destined for psychiatry.

'Quite so! Oh, God! I took him as a favour to his father – I've known the old boy for years – we've met up at meetings all over Europe… You had better start the ward-round without me – I have one or two things to sort out. Gonorrhoea, syphilis and chlamydia, you say?'

'Yes, Sir!'

The boss joined the ward-round ten minutes later. The young doctor was never seen again.

What the boss's wife knew[38]:

I'll take up the narrative here – God knows what happened to the girl, it was probably just business, we'll never know, but the boy – well, you won't get the truth out of that young man – he will have edited the events to his own advantage – proper little opportunist he was – shouldn't have been born tall and handsome – he had enough privilege as it was. He could have put it all down to innocence, naivety but he would never have admitted to that. 'A lot of fuss about nothing!' that will have been his line but probably not even that. He will have told his family that his attachment was unsatisfactory for some reason (he won't have much liked being managed by Mike's lady houseman – that's for sure). He will

....

38. *I don't know what she knew – the italics in this case denote confabulation – I hate loose ends.....*

151

say that he found a way to extract himself from that hole in the slums of London to a more congenial environment – which, in fact, is what he did.

Mike was my first husband, it was his problem really, but wayward sons of international colleagues, like his own children, were woman's work, evidently. He phoned me up at work and asked me to come and collect the young offender – to take him home indeed! What a nerve! To our house – I had to put him up for three days. It was me who had to sort out his spot of bother. I'm a GP in St John's Wood not a venereologist. Anyway, I wasn't about to do it myself – I took him to a Special Clinic in Hendon, in a prefab building hidden behind the hospital. The young man's English wasn't really up to it, so I went in with him just to give the history. I wasn't intending to stay with him. I told the strange, wizened, little man in the grubby white coat and pebbly glasses what the problem was, I had barely said my say before he nodded his scabby head in the direction of the boy's flies and the offending organ was lolloped out and swabs were being taken. No word or eye contact with either of us, just a man in rubber gloves doing his distasteful job as quickly as possible. He handed me the prescription, I thanked the doctor who didn't even look up then and we left.

On the way home I did start to feel a bit sorry for the lad – after all it was a bit humiliating being taken to the doctor by one's boss's wife – like a child. I said, 'That wasn't very nice, was it?'

'In my country, is no big deal!' He said, 'Don't worry.' Well, I wasn't exactly worried. Had it been up to me I would have sent him home with a nasty discharge and told his father exactly why – but Mike is not like that.

Anyway, the long and the short of it is that he went up to Manchester where Mike knew a urologist who owed him a favour and where he was certainly less likely to fall into temptation. It wasn't long before we heard that he had got a visa for the US – perhaps he had stepped out of line there too and got himself moved on. Mike and I divorced a few years later (he ran off and married one of his students). One of my sons told me though that they were still in contact with the father and the last report was that he, the son with the STDs, was a professor of urology somewhere in California – already onto his third wife! Doubtless two divorces will have been expensive – ironically, just another aspect of sex for money!

What worried me about that whole episode was the way that everyone was outraged (because it was discussed) but the outrage was all related to the 'profession' – what about the girl? That is what I wanted to know – who cared about that kid. Why was she in that situation – that was her story – what was her future?

*

Meanwhile, the doors of the hospital were never locked. In those days there were no 'homeless people' sleeping on the streets but there were 'tramps' – men with long tangled beards and mud coloured skin who wore an inordinate number of smelly overcoats. They moved around from place to place keeping out of sight at night, I had heard them in the areas (the sunken yards giving access to the basements) of the derelict houses opposite our old student rooms. There they would drink meths and argue noisily late at night. Reputedly they favoured the brick arches of the London marshalling yards but occasionally one would be spotted, asleep, sitting on the floor, his back propped against a wall in the service area of the hospital. Sometimes an offering of food was left beside him – best not wake him.

One night I was in the private ward, this comprised a series of single rooms off a long corridor – allegedly these could be rented by patients as 'amenity' beds where you could be away from the bustle of the general wards and could be forgotten for days. It usually served as a useful pool of gender non-aligned beds for the overflow from other wards. The patient I had come to see had been admitted as an overflow from another hospital's A&E as someone who had airways obstruction due to a thyroid swelling. The ward was shrouded in darkness and silence.

I was perplexed – standing at the end of a bed in which a lady with rapid stertorous breathing was lying, propped in a cone of light from a single bulb above her head. Her hair was long and black and gathered into one long plait and she spoke a language that no-one understood – the only history that I had managed to obtain was from her 7-year-old son who had said that she had a 'bean in her neck' and had already been seen by several doctors. He had also shown me the thyroxine tablets that his mother took. I had noted the thyroid swelling which was regular and non-tender. An interpreter had eventually been found

153

on the other side of Brent – yes, it was definitely 'a bean, like a gland, she speaks a very peculiar dialect…' Or was it 'gland like a bean – definitely in her neck.' She had stridor, narrowing of her airway which caught her breath in every inspiration. This was associated with considerable agitation. I would do blood gases – not a simple matter. It involved walking about a mile and fiddling with a huge, bad-tempered machine – not to mention stabbing the poor, terrified woman in her groin and finding a nurse who could be relied upon to press hard on the puncture site for 15 minutes. If the oxygen saturation was impaired, I would transfer her to the thoracic surgery unit down the road. Meanwhile I would have another listen to her chest. As I bent over the woman's body to listen with my stethoscope, I turned my head a little and caught sight of the man crouched in the corner of the room. I did not jump because, at first, I thought he was a shadow. I looked hard at him – tall and very thin with a bizarre topknot of tangled hair bundled into a strange, knitted hat, his eyes were closed, he was squatting with his feet flat on the floor and his back against the wall with his knees up to his chin and his head resting back on the cushion of his own headgear – he appeared to be asleep. I straightened myself and slowly rolled up my stethoscope and put it in my pocket – nodded to the patient and very quietly left the room. There was no-one in the sister's office – the ward was empty. I lifted the phone, 'Pranal – there's an intruder in the private ward – propped up sleeping in the corner of room 6 – a young guy.'

'I'm on it!'

'And put me through to the thoracic unit – we've got an urgent transfer… I had made my mind up what to do.

The lady made it to the unit where the senior thoracic surgical registrar attempted to remove the bean with a bronchoscope, it was a borlotti bean, bouncing up and down in her right main bronchus. It had been difficult and there were complications. Sadly, the lady died.

And the angel of death? He had slipped away un-noticed when the ambulance men and the porter and the night sister all arrived, with bells clanging and doors banging.

On paper, I had done everything I should have done but it would haunt me for evermore. In the end the diagnosis was so simple but it had taken so long. Patients will tell you what is wrong with them if you take your time and listen properly – even to a 7-year-old child. Ten minutes after I had arranged the transfer my boss, (a dab hand with a scope) had put his head around the door of sister's office, his wife was with him, they were dressed up and on their way to the Royal College for a dinner, 'Everything alright Di?'

'Yes Sir, we've got a lady with an obstructed airway but she's off to the Thoracic Unit.

'Do you want me to have a look?'

His wife looked accusingly at him then at me.

'No, I think we are okay.'

If the lady had died on the table at Cricklewood Memorial under the experienced hand of Mike Muir, the Coroner would have worried that things might have turned out better in a specialised unit – you never know – that's the trouble with medicine.

Chapter 25.

House Physician

The word meritocracy had been coined in 1958, but the unbiased assessment of merit was to be a long time coming into the medical profession – medical appointments were made according to a system of nepotism based on personal recommendation, racism ('keeping the melanocrit[39] down') and personal preferences (absence of facial hair, suede shoes or a northern accent). It was well recognised that the Dean of the Medical School, a lady, always had the houseman who was the boy with the highest mark for sexual charisma.

'Sir?' I said to my boss over our usual working breakfast, 'May I give your name as a reference for my next job?'

'Of course, where do you want to go?'

'I rather thought I'd like to stay here.'

At that moment in walked Dr Haig the consultant physician, in whose job I was interested.

'Morning Ewart,' said my then boss. 'You'll have this young woman as your next dog's body won't you – she comes highly recommended – properly house-trained!'

'Love to – I like a bit of continuity, we were rather hoping that Phil might stay on as well.'

'Yes, please Sir!' said Phil tucking into bacon and eggs.

'Good! That's settled then – don't talk with your mouth full, Lad.'

Come the new year Phil and I didn't even have to change our on-call bedrooms – just our wards – two large Nightingale wards, one male and one female (the former included a four bedded, unisex, coronary care/intensive therapy unit). 'ITU' was a bit of an over-statement but it did have four beds and a cardiac monitor, that was all, and the four nurses who looked after the male ward and the ITU at night were unusual in that they did permanent nights (two on/two off) – a staffing level that was high relative to the rest of the hospital. They were large and slow-moving women in white uniforms who came on duty like

39. *Portmanteau medical slang word used in the 60s and 70s made from Melanin (skin pigment chemical) and -crit a medical suffix meaning to gauge.*

galleons except that the large white objects that seemed to bear them in were not sails but two large pillows a piece, one under each arm. They would do their medicine round, push a couple of armchairs out of the day room then turn the lights off and snuggle down 'til morning in their nest of pillows.

One night I was surprised to find one of the patients sitting at the sister's desk in the middle of the ward in the middle of the night. He was an anxious man who had been admitted for complete bed rest and a peptic ulcer diet – that is what they did before H2 blocker drugs were developed. Before that time people quite often died from spectacular haemorrhages and perforations caused by their stomach ulcers. If rest and diet didn't work, which quite often they did not, patients might have a vagotomy (cutting of the nerve to the stomach that stimulated acid production) or even a highly selective vagotomy – known by all as 'a highly suggestive vagotomy'. I digress – it all changed almost over-night when the new medical treatment came in, but that would not be for a couple more years.

I checked the patient I had come to see, a Polish seaman with a terribly severe and as yet imprecisely diagnosed chest infection – I checked his intra-venous drip, a cocktail of antibiotics was running in smoothly, but he was not as yet responding. I would give him a couple of hours then check him again. It was as I was leaving that I noticed the man at sister's desk. 'What are you doing there Mr Jenkins?'

'Watching over that poor sod – no one else will – I didn't mean you, Doc!' he said nodding towards the snoozing nurses. 'I'm a baker – I know dough when I see it!' Then looking back at the patient. 'He's been restless and pulling off his oxygen mask – I've just been putting it back.'

'Not very restful for you – you'd better go back to bed – he seems fairly settled at the moment – I'm coming back in a couple of hours to see how he's getting on – we've got to give the treatment a while to work... You know that's your trouble, don't you? I bet you take on everyone else's responsibilities.'

Two nights later I was on the ward and Mr Jenkins caught my eye. 'Psst Doc!'

'Hello!'

'I worry about you and Phil – you work all day and most of the night – I know there isn't a canteen at night, so my wife has bought you in a little supper, I've put it on a tray in the sluice – mum's the word!' he tapped the side of his nose.

For the rest of his stay in hospital a supper was laid for the houseman on duty, every night – a sausage roll or a scotch egg, potato salad and a little pot of pickle, carrot cake or sometimes a gingerbread man.

One of Phil's patients who came to my notice was Dwain, an athletic looking black man in his 20s who suffered from severe and brittle, type 1 diabetes. A nice-natured, friendly young man, one could not really avoid noticing him as he had such dramatic hypos. When his blood sugar dropped precipitately, he would run amuck, escaping from the hospital and sprinting towards the High Street in his pyjamas. The local ambulance service knew him well and, to date, had always managed to round him up, wrestle him to the ground, inject him with glucose and bring him sticky and muddied back to the ward.

One morning on my way to work, I caught sight of Dwain walking briskly down a side street. I stopped the car, double parking, and jumped out, grabbing the tin of barley sugars from the glove compartment and gave chase. I knew not to alarm him by grabbing him or coming at him from behind, so I tore along on the other side of the road then crossed over to approach him from the front, my arms outstretched as if herding geese.

'Hi, Dwain – would you like a sweetie.' I rattled the tin. 'I've got my car here, would you like a ride?'

'You work at the hospital, don't you,' said Dwain who was not wearing his usual striped pyjama – he was dressed as if for work, with polished shoes and socks, I noticed – strange.

'Have a barley sugar,' I said, opening the tin.

'Don't mind if I do,' he said taking one and smiling, 'but I won't get into your car, you're not going my way and anyway I'm not Dwain – I'm Dean – I'm his twin brother – identical, except that I'm not diabetic!

*

It was odd that both Phil and I had a surprisingly tolerant attitude to things that we saw that were wrong where we worked – it didn't really occur to either of us to try to change what we saw. The night-nurses probably had large families that kept them busy all day, they were probably not very well qualified and on pitifully low wages and their patterns of working (or not working) were long established. We two housemen observed the situation, we laughed about it, we mentioned it in passing to our bosses (who certainly knew about it) but it never crossed our minds that we should do anything about it.

Not so with the two new house-surgeons. When Phil and I had done the same jobs, we had very soon worked out that the surgical registrar was a complete waste of space and that our job was to protect the patients from him at all costs (it was a silent understanding between ourselves and the consultants) and it was not difficult as the registrar was as idle as he was ignorant. The only reason he was there was that no decent candidate could be found, and the hospital needed a surgical registrar to be in post to be allowed to function.

The new housemen were of a new breed, assertive women with a very modern sense of entitlement – they were not going to be told what to do by a complete idiot – war was declared – the boat was rocked – dossiers were kept – managers were informed – consultants were edgy – medical defence unions were consulted. Phil and I almost felt sorry for the surgical registrar who was quite old and was obviously never going to progress as a surgeon. The situation was becoming untenable when one of the bosses suggested that the registrar might apply for one of the new posts of A&E consultant in the Midlands, a post where, Phil and I thought, unfettered he could really do some harm. The candidate was reluctant (he had a wife and family in London) – he saw himself as a proper surgeon, not a glorified casualty officer. Pressure was brought to bear – references could be given… Or not.

He got the job.

'Perhaps it'll be mainly administrative – you know – rotas and medical reports,' said Phil.

'He'll have the juniors doing all the real work anyway,' said his colleague.

'Hopefully!'

One of a series of Medical Registrars was another case entirely – quick, clever, hard-working and confident but, I thought, potentially even more dangerous than our previous mentor but in a very subtle way. He had trained in another part of the UK, a city infamous for its religious divisions and I didn't know to which camp in that benighted city he belonged. Whichever it was, he was blessed with complete moral certainty – always dangerous! "Time wasters" were to be discouraged – whether occupying a valuable bed with an overdose or lingering too long at the pearly gates.

His treatment of vulnerable young patients (to teach them a lesson) was harsh and not unusual at that time – he thrust a great wide red-rubber tube down their gullet to wash them out with buckets of warm water, syphoning it in and syphoning it out and talking over their gagging and spluttering. He treated them, mainly young girls with shitty lives, as if they were so much meat or a blocked drain as he joked to the others in the room and triumphantly counted the pale blue and red capsules (Tuinal – the barbiturate of choice that year) as they bobbed up into the bucket on the floor. He gave them tips on more efficient methods of suicide (for next time) quoting the statistics for attempted suicide (dismissing it as a manipulative act rather than a death wish). Then he left them wet, bedraggled and wrapped in a damp blanket in a cold corridor to wait hours for assessment by a proper psychiatrist – all too late. I had watched this during the previous six months, had seen the effect of his bravado on the housemen and the students under his tutelage – seen the effect on the culture of the place. I had seen him send male students to listen to a young lady's chest 'who had interesting physical signs' (lovely breasts!). At first, I am ashamed to admit that I had felt it a bizarre privileged to be included (as neither man nor woman but a lady doctor – the third gender![40]) This it appeared was medicine – new and exciting – all very amusing and grown up – or was it?

Euthanasia had not been discussed at medical school except to point out that strong narcotics like morphine and heroin could be used for pain relief in hopeless cases even though they undoubtedly did shorten life. I heard pneumonia referred to as 'the old man's friend' and one wise old consultant when faced with a suffering and incurable patient would say. 'Make him comfortable, Sister,' then as a quiet aside to the rest of the staff. 'We should not strive officiously in this case.'

40. That was a saying then, if a man had qualms about being seen by a female doctor. 'She's not a woman. There are three genders –men, women and lady doctors.'

That attitude must have gone out of fashion when doctors' hours were reduced and continuity of care was lost – since then very often doctors and nurses treat first and think whether they ought to later, or not at all. I had always thought that vets confronted death much better than doctors – that's not to say that I was ever an advocate of mercy killing – I was not. God, I was noticing, usually took people when they were ready and at that point one should not necessarily strive to keep them alive just because you could – people deserve at least as much consideration as a much-loved pooch.   However, actually putting them to sleep (knowing the impatience of some doctors, nurses and relatives) was to stretch the analogy too far.

I was absorbing the attitudes of the time, but those times were changing, though I was not ready to take on the medical establishment (even locally). I heard my registrar telling a patient how to end their life more efficiently next time so as not to waste his time which might well have been a negative injunction[41]. I heard him making impressionable young doctors think that the power of life and death could be in their hands and teaching them the science, if not the practice, of how to hasten death without being found out (or so he thought). This convinced me that lines had to be drawn but I did not feel guilty about not confronting his assertions or reporting this brash, young registrar at the time. I suppose I thought it all bravado which it probably was. Decades later when Harold Shipman, a General Practitioner, was found guilty of the multiple murder of vulnerable (possibly heart-sink[42]) patients, I remembered that registrar, and was not entirely surprised that it could happen.

What shaped my view on end-of-life care was more to do with what was happening at home. My Uncle Peter (of the carbolic and whisky) was dying of pancreatic cancer – then it carried a hopeless prognosis and he had already survived an amazing six months. On three occasions he was on the point of death, once with pneumonia (the old man's friend) when Mum called the doctor because his breathing was so difficult, and she didn't know what to do – he was admitted to hospital and treated intensively so that he could return home. A couple

41. *Telling someone to do the opposite of what you want them to do.*
42. *A term used in the medical literature for patients who make their doctor's heart sink when they come into the consulting room.*

of weeks later he became comatose and Mum called the doctor again – he was admitted to hospital and the power of modern medicine was again invoked – his septicaemia, due to a urinary infection this time, was aggressively treated so that he could go home again so he could (as I said) get something even worse. Some weeks later he had a stroke – he unconscious again – he was a big man and Mum could not roll him to keep him dry and clean. This time, rather than seeing him off in the ambulance then cycling back to her own home weeping tears of remorse and relief, Mum had some moral support. This time she and I went with him to the hospital to sit with him and to challenge the worst excesses of medical enthusiasm and the desire to free up beds (this was the beginning of the era of 100% bed occupancy) – we reassured each doctor, as they came to assess him, that there was no pressure for active treatment on our part – the poor man, he was seventy-nine, had suffered enough. When his pneumonia inevitably ensued, a now more confident junior doctor explained to us that he thought perhaps they should avoid prolonging his suffering but make him comfortable – which they did, and he died peacefully the following day.

Uncle Peter had been important to me, I loved him, he was like a spare dad – he had always been proud of me and pleased to see me. Batchelor uncles and spinster aunts who stayed at home most of their lives seemed to be a feature of family life then and were great assets to their families. He had bought me my first car, after I had admitted to him my motor bike debacle with the police officer on Barnet Hill – I had meant it as an amusing anecdote, not as a bid for a second-hand Hillman Imp, but was nevertheless grateful when it arrived.

Some year's previously he had developed a strange high stepping gait and was having a lot of falls and black-outs and driving his car (yes, that's right) very slowly and deliberately. He was not a man to complain – his default position on illness was one of denial. Mum and I were worried, but despite being sent to consult his doctor nothing seemed to change. I had visited the Institute of Neurology as a student and wished I could take him there. One afternoon each week all the neurology senior registrars in the London area gathered in a tiered, oak panelled lecture theatre in this historic institution in Queen's Square, where a senior consultant would see interesting and mysteriously ill patients and they would all brainstorm and discuss and be amazed by the cleverness and experience of that particular doyen of the profession. On one occasion I, as a neurophysiology student, had been allowed to sneak into the back row and listen.

I thought well why not and phoned the hospital and asked how to go about getting him seen – a nice lady had simply told me to come at 2pm on Tuesday and bring my uncle in some loosely fitting clothes with a sample of urine and copies (if possible) of any blood tests that his GP might have done. When we arrived, Peter in his new over-sized track suit was ushered in and I was invited to join him and sit in the front row – he said he didn't mind, so I did.

It was like a Victorian etching or an old Punch cartoon, he lay on a leather examination couch in the cock pit of the amphitheatre while Sir Roger Bannister,[43] world famous inside and outside medicine, put him through his paces. Questions and answers ricocheted around the theatre and young men came down into the arena to elucidate and demonstrate various physical signs and to question the patient and me. They stood him up and walked him up and down with murmurs of satisfaction. They pushed him and pulled him and told him to close his eyes and did it again – they caught him when he toppled over. They hit him with hammers and pricked him with pins, shone lights into his eyes and asked him some very personal questions which he answered without the slightest hesitation. At the end the nature of his diabetes and his peripheral neuropathy was explained to him by the great man and the relationship of both of these to his high alcohol consumption and his associated liver disease. Sir Roger Bannister advised him to stop drinking alcohol and that it would all probably improve though not necessarily completely. This he did and it did. As far as I know he never took another drink – on the way home he thanked me and we never mentioned it again. This had been a very powerful dose of doctor!

---

43. First man to run a mile in less than 4 minutes. In 1954 he broke the record with a time of 3min 59.4 sec helped by Christopher Chataway and Chris Brasher all of whom became household names. He then had an equally distinguished but less well-known career in medicine.

My reward? From very early in my career I could always sniff out a closet drinker and diabetic keto-acidosis and I always felt a secret affinity for alcoholics.

Sadly, although Peter forswore alcohol for a number of years before he died the damage to the cells of his pancreas must already have been done.

Chapter 26.

Vocational Training.

Having spent some time in the district general hospital in my hometown visiting poor Peter, when I noticed that they were advertising their innovative vocational training for GPs in the BMJ.[44] I couldn't wait to tell Phil.

'You should apply for this Phil!'

'But...'

'It's a really friendly little hospital with loads of bread-and-butter medicine and it would be a really good area for you and Carol to settle – good schools – lots of new houses – and you'd be just the good GP that I'd like to look after my mum and dad in their dotage!'

'Vocational training isn't mandatory until the end of next year.'

'No, but you don't want to start out being in the second division with all the young chaps coming up being better qualified than you... If you get into a training scheme before everyone is forced to do it you'll be in a much better position when it comes to applying for partnerships.'

'You're a bully, you! I've got such a lot to do – when is the closing date.'

So it was that Phil and Carol moved to Hertfordshire.

It also set me thinking – mandatory vocational training next year. I had been planning to do an SHO job at the renal unit in Hampstead in which I had worked as a student – it was pretty well arranged but the career progress of a physician was to be long and it might well be interrupted by moves related to Angus's career and childbirth and God knows what else – there might well be times in my life when a bit of part-time general practice could be very useful. Perhaps I should be thinking about at least getting the most taxing bits of a vocational training under my belt before I had any children.

The following week I was running up the stairs at Hadley General Hospital, two at a time, trying to keep up with the tall, young, dynamic gynaecologist who worked there, Harvey Brightman. After a tip off from his secretary I had ambushed him at the foot of the main staircase

44. *British Medical Journal*

and was breathlessly telling him why I would like to work for him and asking him if we might explore that possibility.

'Are you pregnant?'

'No'

'Can you start on the first of next month?'

'Yes.' We had reached the top of the stairs.

'Then give your details to my secretary – I'll see you on the 1st.'

'But…?'

He was about to disappear into a ward, I had held back a little, but he turned and over his shoulder he shouted. 'Congratulations – you've got the job!' Then he vanished.

I spent the next six months in the bright new obstetric unit at the top of Hadley Hill as part of a team that worked together to make the experience of childbirth as safe and as pleasant as possible for the initially nervous but thereafter grateful ladies of the borough and their even more nervous and much younger looking husbands – funny that. The registrars were competent and not in the least predatory and the midwives were young and friendly and not in love with any of the doctors. All was presided over by a senior midwife, Miss Monisha, of whom everyone except the patients was terrified – she was often on the labour ward herself, delivering babies, and knew absolutely everything that was going on. The consultants – an Indian, an Englishman and a Jew all seemed to get on well, at least they talked to each other and they ran any changes past Miss Monisha before introducing them. Private practice which only involved the gynaecology was not a problem as they all drew their private patients from different demographics (only royalty or the super-rich or super-dumb had their babies privately for reasons that I understood only too well[45]).

I delivered quite a few babies myself, more than enough to qualify to sit for a diploma of the Royal College of Obstetricians and Gynaecologists (DRCOG) after taking the exam at the end of the post. At each delivery I would find my eyes filling with tears at the recognition of a new life – no one seemed to mind (it was better than fainting which is what a lot of the Dad's seemed to want to do – I was learning to be aware of wobbling spectators in my peripheral vision.

45. See Chapter 8 – Evie's account of the perinatal death of her firstborn in a private hospital.

Obstetrics is the art of judging what is normal and will progress to a successful outcome and what is not. As with most natural processes, I learned it is best not to intervene in childbirth unless it is really necessary. The more healthy, rested and relaxed a mother is the more likely it is to go well. So convinced of this was my boss, that he was keen to do a clinical trial of marijuana in the first stage of labour – only for the patients (not the staff) and only for those who usually used the drug to relax – it would be many years (if ever) before any ethics committee would agree to this but it did show that he understood the importance of ambiance in labour!

One of the most memorable confinements that I witnessed was that of an older woman, an academic. She was in a large, assisted delivery suite, because of her age – it was her first child. Her husband sat next to her on a blue plastic chair doing the Times crossword. As she seemed a sensible sort and there was lots of room, we had asked her if she minded a few student nurses watching. About twelve trainee nurses gathered around the end of the bed like a choir – the ones at the back standing on squat stools. They were all dressed in white hospital smocks and with white caps and masks, most for some reason that year had been recruited in South East Asia, and were very new to the UK – it was early in their introduction to nursing. The delivery went well – a large screaming baby deposited itself between the lady's wide-open legs. I lifted the infant still attached to the cord and placed it on the mother's abdomen, all gory, wriggling and screaming healthily for the mother to hold. The mother looked at the miracle in her arms then at the host of shocked, angelic faces gathered around and she shouted 'Smile, won't you! What is wrong with you? Can't you see, I have had a baby! Sing Hallelujah… Or something!'

Not all confinements were so joyful.

That same day a young woman expecting her third child was transferred to the labour ward in suspected early labour – she had had (as they used to say) *a show* – the passage of a little blood-stained mucous which often presages labour. She had been languishing on the antenatal ward for some weeks following some vaginal bleeding which had instigated a scan (rarely done in those days) and what was known as *a high head at term*. The scan had shown the placenta lying where the baby's head should have been, right over the internal os (the way out – the plughole) of the womb. Under these unusual circumstances a mother might be expected to bleed heavily should labour ensue so these unfortunate women were kept under careful observation, with blood for transfusion cross-matched and ready and scans repeated as the baby grew in the vain hope that the placenta would decide to migrate upwards allowing the baby to squeeze past without causing a catastrophic haemorrhage during labour. Otherwise, when the baby was big enough arrangements were made to deliver it by Caesarean section before its head was pushed by an energetic uterus through the vascular placenta (an organ similar to a thick omelette made of delicate blood vessels). This lady had jumped the gun and had started in early labour on a very busy morning – all the assisted delivery rooms were full, and the registrar was already doing a pre-planned Caesarean on another lady with an audience of slightly traumatised student nurses whose notions of the wonders of life were being challenged. Our lady was in the four bedded first-stage room with three other nervous mums-to-be.

I pulled the curtains around the bed and put up a drip (thank goodness) and had started a salbutamol infusion in an endeavour to inhibit her labour, the registrar was still busy with the elective section, and an anaesthetist who would normally have to be called from the General Hospital down the road was already in the building. All this went through my mind as I bent my head over the lady's abdomen with my ear very lightly pressed against my foetal stethoscope (a thing like a small military bugle) listening to the baby's regular heartbeat and gazing absently at the indentation in the lady's mattress. Just then I sensed a change –a hardening of the woman's tummy – she had started a contraction, the first one – a 'good' one, I prepared to wait for it to end as the indentation of the mattress around the patient filled in an instant with blood – its iridescent surface swirling with a thousand sparkles. The patient looked puzzled for a moment. 'There's something warm,' she said feeling the side of her thigh with her hand then holding it up dripping blood. 'Oh my God!'

I pushed the emergency button by the bed producing a gratifying stampede of midwives including Miss Monisha – it was imperative to get the patient into theatre and the baby out before the next contraction. I took a bag of cold blood from one of the midwives, checked the name and fixed it to the giving set as the bed was manoeuvred out of the room with the patient in it. Miss Monisha shouted for a blood warmer and a pump, the lady now the same colour as her pillow was losing consciousness. I raised the blood drip as high as it would go but the flow was inadequate, I climbed onto the bed and squeezed the bag, that was better, I squeezed harder – there was a red-out!

The force had pushed the spike of the giving set out of the bag which had squirted precious cold blood all over me, turning my glasses into sheets of sticky blood. I snatched them off and reattached the giving set with my slippery hands as Miss Monisha passed me the pump, which was basically a blood pressure cuff made to pump up around the blood bag. I attached it and Miss Monisha pumped as I held the whole thing together while balancing on the moving bed.

As we crashed into the operating theatre the flotilla of white clad student-nurses, waiting uneasily since the last case, scattered like seagulls to roost around the edges of the room, pressed, startled, against the walls by the aura of urgency. When blood is spilled on green theatre scrubs and drapes, they just look wet. When it is spread generously on ordinary white bed sheets it is much more dramatic and when sprayed from a great height onto an ordinary, white-coated medic, it is spectacular – to their credit none of the students fainted or ran away and the lady-anaesthetist immediately covered the patient with green towels as she was lifted onto the table. I noted with relief three more units of blood on the anaesthetist's trolley.

I rapidly went and changed into theatre scrubs, covering my bloody hair with a theatre cap. Miss Monisha joined me in the nurses changing room and, saying nothing, wet a swab under the tap and dabbed at my face. 'We can't have you looking like Sweeny Todd, Dr Grant.'

'Thank you, Miss Monisha.'

Re-entering the fray, I took my place at the theatre table in time to hold out a dressing towel to receive a rather limp, blue infant. I cradled it firmly in my arms and turned to take it to the resuscitaire, an inclined plane on which babies could be laid, head down, for intubation and resuscitation. The paediatrician was nowhere to be seen having left the hospital following the previous case moments before this had all kicked off. I sucked the mucous from the baby's little mouth with a sucker – the infant was still not breathing although I could feel its little heart beating rapidly against its chest wall. I had intubated babies before but my first instinct was to put my own mouth over the babe's and, holding its nose give it some little puffs of air – I could feel it's chest rising and falling as I did this. Immediately the infant reacted (I could feel it). I straightened up and it let out a glorious cry and I held an oxygen mask lightly over its face so that between yells it gasped in the oxygen and a pinkness spread over its waxy premature skin.

'What is it?' shouted the registrar.

'Alive!' I said, looking at the baby now kicking off its covering. 'It's a girl!'

Then as if to myself. 'That's good.' By way of explanation, to the little group of be-gowned and be-masked student nurses that had gathered behind me: 'Females are more resistant to anoxia. We females are the basic utility model – more robust. Men are the sports version. More enjoyable, use more fuel and break down a lot!' A sea of blank faces looked back at me.

'Blood pressure's coming up at last,' said the anaesthetist.

'That's parenthood for you!' said the registrar remembering his audience. 'You know what they say girls: the third stage of labour lasts the rest of your life!' Several of the students wrote this down while the other staff all groaned.

*

This was not to be the last time that I was wheeled into theatre from the labour ward. The next time it was with another *high head at term*. (Lessons to be learned here!) The lady was in labour but not progressing very well and the baby's head had not engaged in the pelvis as it is supposed to do in the last weeks of pregnancy. The scan had not shown *placenta previa* on this occasion and the baby was overdue but there was a plan. I was to persuade the head to engage (which could be done) by pushing down on it from the top, while the registrar (at the business end) ruptured the membranes – letting out lots of fluid and encouraging the baby's head to come down into the birth canal and the uterus to push more effectively. This was a procedure not without risk as I was about to find out.

The lady was very long suffering and good humoured (which was as well). I was busy pushing her baby's head down into her pelvis as the registrar, Raj, fumbled out of sight. There was a gush of water from the vagina which seemed to go on and on and I could feel a contraction and was thinking *that should do it.*

'Shit!' said the registrar. 'Nurse, call the duty anaesthetist and the paediatrician ASAP and bring in a trolley.'

Then to the patient. 'Can you roll onto your tummy, that's right, I'm keeping my hand where it is for a very good reason, now draw your knees up under your bottom and can you get your chest flat on the bed.'

'Oh, we did this in yoga – it's called melting heart,' said the lady, unfazed – I was wide eyed and puzzled.

'Now Di, put on a glove, I want you to climb up on the bed, here, behind what's-your-name-again?'

'Melanie.'

'Behind Melanie, and slip your hand in, under mine, that's it. You can feel the presenting part, I'll ease my hand out, there's plenty of room can you feel the cord there on the left?'

'Yes, it's quite high – I can feel a pulsation.'

'That is very good – you've got to hold the head like that and prevent that loop of cord coming out any further, we don't want the head squashing the cord – gravity should help you in that position.'

'I understand – are you alright Melanie?'

'You see Melanie,' continued Raj. 'You have a very long cord, and it is trying to get out before the baby which is not good – we're going to take you to theatre for an emergency Caesarean section but in the meantime, it may be undignified, but Dr Grant here is going to hold the cord out of harm's way till we get this baby out, okay?'

'Okay!'

At that moment, the trolley arrived. 'You girls are young enough and agile enough to climb across onto this trolley keeping the same yoga pose – okay?'

'Okay!' and we did. At that point we were both covered with a bed sheet and wheeled out into the busy corridor and along to the theatre.

'This is surreal!' I whispered.

'No stranger than conception!' replied Melanie.

Raj was a very experienced and slick surgeon and as the spinal anaesthetic started to work, Melonie was flipped carefully over with me still attached. In moments the baby was out, I retained all my digits and was able to receive little Liam, who was pink and wrinkly and shouted a lot which delighted his mother, whose eyes filled with tears of joy as, of course, did mine.

Later in the tea-room, where we were joined by the boss, Raj admitted that in a lot of hospitals they would have done an elective section straight away without risking an induction. The boss added that with less experienced staff Caesarean section is easier and safer than other less practiced procedures!

'You are kidding!' I said. 'It doesn't look easy to me.'

'That reminds me,' said the boss. 'Because you juniors could end up anywhere – in the Hebrides, cut off in a storm – on a cruise ship stuck in a war zone – preaching your particular gospel in the heart of Africa, it is important that you can all do a Caesarean Section. Therefore, I make it a rule that you all do at least one while you work for me – I'll look out for a suitable case for you Di – nothing complicated. So, you had better concentrate while you are assisting – right?

'Oh my God!'

'Are you not contemplating a career in obstetrics?' asked Raj. 'You have a nice way with the patients.'

'No, I am not!' I said emphatically. 'Babies are far too precious, and obstetrics is far too scary.'

*

Harvey Brightman was a man of his word, that word might well be laced with *double entendre* and delivered with the blunt innuendo that was a sign of the times, but I did not consider him flirtatious – just an ageing bachelor (he was in his late thirties) trying to sound as if he didn't live with his mother.

'Mrs Khan is listed for elective section on Tuesday, it's her fourth child after a long gap, she's forty with old spinal damage (small pelvis – big baby) – ideal case for you! I'll hold your hand.'

'I'll cross match four units of blood!' (Two was the norm.)

'You won't be needing blood!' and that fortunately was the case. I was, and more importantly Mrs Khan was, safely steered through a

Caesarean section, every stitch of which would be indelibly ingrained on my memory for all time – truly ready to access when next I was trapped on a cruise ship in a war zone.

'I won't be home tonight Angus – I'd rather be here, just in case.'

'But you aren't on call.'

'No, but there is a lady I want to keep a special eye on – if she bleeds, I need it to be spotted straight away.'

'But… '

'I did her Caesarean section today, Angus. Single handed (well Harvey watched).'

'Christ – they let you do the whole thing – you'd better stay!'

'Thanks Angus!' I said with irony.

*

It was Christmas. It was the end of my post. We, the obstetric team, were having a party at a local hostelry at Harvey's expense. Angus (though he hated that sort of thing) had joined us. It was a jokey atmosphere and thinking he should enter into the spirit of the evening Angus regaled the company with my latest domestic disaster – the flooding of the kitchen during my attempts to unblock the washing machine filter blocked by hair grips and one of his many odd socks. Everyone laughed except Harvey – his expression hardened. 'It's a miracle that she finds the time to wash your socks – you perhaps don't appreciate what a talented, hard-working doctor you have the good fortune to have doing your laundry.'

I had never thought of Harvey as a feminist!

Chapter 27.

A career is a retrospective concept

I did have a sort of plan – to get the most taxing, challenging part of my training (for whatever it was I would eventually do) over and done with early. To this end I spoke to the consultant paediatrician at Hadley – a fatherly figure who seemed quite interested in the idea of me working there – the hospital had just lost its recognition for the training of career paediatricians and he had been wondering where on earth his next houseman was coming from. I explained that what I was interested in was paediatrics in the context of general practice and the fact that they didn't have enough in-patient throughput and hardly any intensive care was not a problem for me – in fact it was an asset (I had already worked out that I did not want to spend my life caring for critically ill babies – far too scary). I wanted to see lots of normal children (normal is always a good starting point) and those with everyday ordinary complaints. I wanted to be able to assess risk – understand just how ill a child was with asthma or meningitis and to hand over the really poorly ones quickly to someone else. I wanted to be able to judge development, learn how to manage fits and treat bed-wetting.

'I think there is the germ of an idea here,' said the Paediatrician. 'There's someone I'd like you to talk to.'

Next, I spoke to the post-graduate dean who was also wrestling with the recruitment problems of a district general hospital, living in the shadow of many teaching hospitals and post-graduate institutes that mopped up all the interesting cases and all the talent. It seemed that no-one had been thinking about the needs of trainee GPs but perhaps this was the answer – the Hadley General GP training scheme was conceived – I (with six months start on the rest) was to be its first alumna.

For six months I wrestled with the perennial paediatric dilemmas – whether infants with croup (a narrowing of the airways that makes them sound like doors, squeaking in the wind of their own respiration) had viral tracheitis (which is common and gets better by itself) or

174

epiglottitis (which presents in the same way but deteriorates rapidly with dire consequences). Not being able to distinguish between these two conditions had been a source of much litigation in the past. I learned how to do this with confidence tempered with caution – I saw enough children with the real thing to know when to be alarmed and when to be reassuring. It would be another sixteen years before a vaccine would render this skill redundant.

The same went for meningitis – I laid my hand on every fontanelle[46] that crossed my path so that when my boss diagnosed a rare listeria meningitis with little in the way of illness but a boggy fontanelle – I too could feel the difference and might know it next time. Never more would I be able to pass an infant without resting my hand on its head.

My days were punctuated by frantic dashes up the road to resuscitate newborn babies at the maternity unit – I soon had a notion of the skill of the various agents of Hypnos (anaesthetists) involved in delivering oblivion to the mothers during obstetric procedures. Their accomplishments were variable and there were occasions when I suspected the hand of Thanatos (twin brother of the aforementioned) whose remit was death. Fortunately, I soon realised that newborn babies were more robust than one might imagine. On a more practical level I was so familiar with the ancient kit in the obstetric department that I knew exactly how to keep my pelvis pressed against the resuscitaire at all times while dealing with babies who would not breathe that at no time did one ever slide off the inclined plain of the table to be caught, or not caught, by an attendant midwife who was also familiar with the quirks of the equipment.

The rest of the time I spent in the outpatients' department listening to parental complaints of too much or too little. Offspring either ate, or slept, or ran about, or talked, or poohed or peed too much or not enough – they were too fat or too thin, too tall or too short or their skin was too greasy or too dry. Thus, I familiarised myself with the wide parameters of normality and the amazing diversity of a North London population.

*

I had a very high opinion of the man for whom I worked, he was near retirement and exuded a calm wisdom entirely in keeping with the

46. *The soft part of a baby's head where the bones of the skull are still to join*

lofty Victorian hospital that had what we now call 'orangery windows' in the roof of the long paediatric ward on the top floor.

One day a bird that had strayed into the ward became trapped, flying up against the glass of one of these windows. Its frantic tweeting was disturbing the ward and distracting the medical students that the boss was trying to teach — it didn't take much to distract a medical student. Now, I knew my boss was an enthusiastic birdwatcher and early twitcher (nothing to do with Twitter — it was long before that). Perhaps I thought I'd impress him, I may even have been a little bit bored.

'I'll get the pole and let that bird out!' I said and went to fetch the thing like a giant boathook that opened the sky lights.

'Good idea!' said he.

When I came back, they had moved along the ward, nearer to the bird and could see the flapping, squawking creature more clearly as it threw itself repeatedly against the glass in panic.

'Oh! It's only a starling!' said the boss. 'Leave it!'

Crash! There it was, shattered on the ground – not the window – not even the bird – but my shattered illusions – my respect, in shards on the floor of a paediatric ward in North London.

Later, when the previously wise old patriarch, now demoted to a racist tyrant, was having his coffee, I went back and released the bird.

There were only two deaths during my tenure as paediatric houseman, both were infants who had been born in the hospital but had never been well enough to go home, both had severe and little understood genetic abnormalities, inborn errors of metabolism, that marred their development and stopped them from thriving – one grew large but still reacted entirely as a floppy new-born baby – the other, the nurses' favourite, remained tiny. Both finally passed away after many agonising months in hospital leaving the parents and staff bereft. I thought about how the parents would now be able to focus on their other children and maybe even have a further pregnancy with a more successful outcome. I wondered briefly if there was something wrong with me for not sharing the nurses' grief and I wondered if I would react in the same way once I had had children of my own. Empathy, I concluded, had to be tempered with common sense.

Paula was a contemporary at medical school, I had observed her from a distance, I had never seen any girl who was so extrovert – short and curvy, she broadcasted her confidence, attractiveness and good humour loudly wherever she was (generally not an endearing quality in other women) – she quite took my breath away. Now Paula was medical registrar to my senior house officer and together with Sally, the houseman, we comprised one of the medical teams at Hadley General Hospital – the 'A' team (according to Paula).

Sally was a girl with a large angular frame swaddled in layers of trendy knitwear to obscure her failing self-esteem, poor body image and plummeting weight. She and her handsome stylish husband drove around, when not working, within another layer of obfuscation – a beautifully presented vintage sports car. As a doctor Sally was not very confident but not afraid to ask me who in turn was happy to run our medical queries past Paula if necessary. Out of hours, Paula sat propped by pillows in the middle of a large double bed in her room in the duty residence with phone in hand, surrounded not by medical reference books (she seemed to have no need of these) but by innumerable and lavishly illustrated cookery books which lay open lasciviously and spilled zucchini, spinach and blue cheese quiche, chocolate, chilly and peanut butter pasta and one hundred and one things to make with pecan nuts all over the bed and onto the floor. From here she co-ordinated the medical take, decisively and competently (phone in hand) – she trusted me to supervise Sally and told me everything I needed to know and she made her decisions about the management of cases quickly and unambiguously although occasionally showing slight vacillation such as: 'No problem, give him IV pen. and strep. (don't forget the bloods) and anti-coagulate with heparin – but Di... I'm not sure about maple syrup with mango, what do you think, is it too sweet?'

'Too heavy, what about honey and balsamic...'

Thus, we bonded. Sally became more confident, Paula stayed in bed at night, doing what she did best, managing. Me. I dashed about happy in the knowledge that I was doing the right thing. Unlike some of my previous registrars, I trusted Paula's judgement in all things medical (though not when it came to men). This was just as well because consultant input was patchy.

The boss, a bright young consultant general physician with an interest in cardiology had experienced some chest pain while mowing his lawn. Being trained in cardiology, rather than resting and waiting to see if it went off, he thought he would finish the mowing and see if that made the pain any worse – it did! He then drove himself to the hospital and did an ECG on himself. Looking at the tracing made his chest hurt even more so he called an ambulance to take him to the National Heart Hospital, arriving just in time to confirm his worst fears by having a cardiac arrest! He was resuscitated but continued to experience, first-hand, all the complications and primitive surgical interventions available in his chosen specialty by 1976 – all before his 43rd birthday.

Meanwhile Paula had the excuse to discuss the management of our cardiac patients with any number of bright young cardiology senior registrars in the area – making her even more up to date in her chosen specialty and getting to know her future colleagues.

When he returned to work his staff monitored his angina by the time it took for the ward round to walk up the incline from the male medical ward to the female. This was a time when men from forty onwards were thought of as 'middle aged' and frequently dropped dead from heart attacks or ruptured aortic aneurysms related to undiagnosed hypertension, raised cholesterol and smoking (often started in the armed forces). The changes that were then afoot in General Practice would change all that –and would tend to make us forget our mortality.

I spent a year in general medicine, six months of which still involved me in catching the babies that were swung from the open abdomens of their mothers up at the maternity unit and saving them from the slippery slope of the resuscitaire and the overenthusiasm of certain junior anaesthetists.

Paula was studying for her MRCP[47] before embarking on a very competitive career in Cardiology, she had booked two weeks study leave.

'Can I get study leave?' I asked.

Not unless I was taking a bona-fide exam, explained the hospital secretary.

47. *Membership of the Royal College of Physicians*

'Take part one with me,' said Paula, 'Most of the fees are refundable – it will cost you about six quid– that's got to be worth it for two weeks off work – we can study together.'

That is what we did, plus a weekend course at the Royal College. I decorated our study and quizzed Paula on her revision –I picked up lots more useful knowledge although I made no pretence at proper study. Paula passed first time with flying colours and, amazingly, I very nearly passed too – I got a 'bare fail' which almost persuaded me to do it again with a little more effort. However, a year in General Practice beckoned.

Chapter 28.

Turned loose on the community

If you are paying attention and have any interest in the preparation of doctors for family practice you will have noticed the gaping deficiency in my vocational training. So far there had only been a cursory and unedifying brush with psychiatry as an undergraduate and my broken pact with the Almighty.[48] Thus, it was arranged that I should start spending time in the psychiatry outpatients at Hadley with the consultant psychiatrist known as Jaz. He was plump, his skin darkish and a bit pot marked, his hair brownish and untidy – his speech uncomplicated, articulate and warm and he had a party trick! This was something that I would spend the rest of my life trying, unsuccessfully, to emulate – in one of the most cosmopolitan boroughs of Greater London, Jaz greeted each and every patient in their mother tongue. He spoke fluent Urdu, Hindi and Swahili (fair enough) but didn't hesitate to enquire about their children in Gujarati, in Punjabi, in Bengali, in Kashmiri or Marathi. When a local Chinese businessman bought his daughter in, they were regaled not in Mandarin or Cantonese but in his native Fujianese. He took the first few moments of any new consultation in getting the patient to tell him how to do this… And remembering. Nobody knew how he did it. He greeted a Barnet milkman in Welsh and a jazz singer in Hausa (complete with clicks!) Five minutes to master the social niceties of their culture and everything else flowed naturally. There were no erect penises lurking behind his curtains – this was proper psychiatry – and genuine interest and love of humanity.

For that training year in general practice, I was to spend my Thursday mornings at the feet of the master watching this plump, friendly man tease out the psychological ills of North London with empathy and common sense peppered with a little pharmacology where necessary.

For the rest of the week, I was attached to a local practice that cared for the people of the council estates of a post-war new town and the leafy lanes of an adjacent village. Here I was nurtured by mentors who had a genuine vocation for family medicine – the senior partner was

48. *Chapter 19 – Granny's leucotomy*

president of the Royal College of General Practitioners. They believed in the importance of being 'independent contractors' to the NHS – taking the money and providing the services that were required and (most importantly) keeping control of their own working environment, employing their own staff and using their own premises. They looked after their own patients, 24 hours a day and 7 days each week. Run well, by someone with a head for business and a heart for their patients, this could produce an efficient and cost-effective service. Like almost everything in those days it relied on good will – provided the contracted practitioners were professional (self-regulating), fair and honest (to the spirit and not just the letter of the contract) it worked swimmingly and allowed great developments in general practice... However, I would soon notice flaws in the system.

The partners in the practice (profit-sharing, fully invested and in control) preached its advantages. The salaried assistants admitted the advantage of not having to invest in, buy into, the practice but did not enjoy the same rewards or control of their workload, they were predominantly women (who the partners would say just wanted to do their work and get home to their families and not have the responsibility of 24/7 patient care). Differential earnings were not discussed. Mmm, thought I.

Aneurin Bevan admitted that to achieve the agreement of the doctors' negotiators when setting up of the NHS he had 'stuffed their mouths with gold'. Politicians have emulated this technique to achieve the more recent renegotiations, particularly of the General Practice contracts. Money is a good driver for change but only so far – there comes a time when the work and responsibilities become so onerous and the rewards have to be so great that the whole nature of the profession is changed. The workload becomes unsustainable, if a reasonable standard is to be maintained, and recruitment becomes almost impossible and selects those more interested in financial than vocation rewards.

My trainer was the youngest of the partners, only a few years older than me, he was balding, bearded and intense. He spent a lot of time teaching me and took me home every few weeks for dinner with his wife who, not surprisingly, was less impressed by the young, lady doctor who was taking up so much of her husband's time! Another partner also invited me home regularly for supper when I was on-call – grilled chicken breast with new potatoes and salad followed by unsweetened, dried fruit salad with prunes and hoops of pale apple (he had recently suffered a heart attack). From the head of his elegant dining room table, he told amusing medical anecdotes that always had a lesson somewhere embedded in the narrative – this was the age of anecdotal learning and I enjoyed the process and the paternalism of the era. As my cynicism grew year on year, I would wonder, thinking back, what tax allowance he had claimed for feeding the on-call trainee or what fee for teaching me. And why not?

General Practitioners on-call in those days depended on a doctor's wife – every doctor needed one. This was another example of how good will kept the wheels turning – and maybe a modest disbursement. I had no wife but Angus was willing, on his nights off to answer the phone. Bearing in mind how hard he worked this must have been an added burden. It seemed quite natural at the time but may have contributed to his reluctance to become embroiled in my preoccupations, domestic and professional, as time went on.

Communication when on-call was primitive. Angus would take calls from patients and pass them on to 'the doctor'. There were no walkie-talkies or mobiles – the doctor would beg to use the telephone as she finished a consultation in a patient's home and would collect the next calls. Very often there was no phone and I would be directed to the nearest public phone box, my pockets jingling with small change. When there were no more calls, I would drive the 20 minutes home to get some sleep by which time another call might well have come in and off I would go again – the alternative was to sit in my car by a phone box hoping that it reliably received incoming calls and that, if it did, I would hear it. This did not work as I would lose my nerve and call in, waking Angus when (for once) the patients had let him sleep. Fortunately, the night work was not onerous and usually tailed off at about 11 pm, after which no one really wants to go out to a phone box to call a doctor. As the partners usually did the night work themselves, patients were generally well trained. When the doctor you saw at night was the very same one you knew, and had seen the day before, and could see the next morning, a degree of self-restraint was exercised, although it didn't always feel like it to me at the time – as continuity of care was eroded by demand, things would only get worse.

It was 3 a.m. and I had just packed a lady off to the hospital in an ambulance – she had suffered a heart attack. Now I drove down the A1 towards the Hadley turn and home when my car lurched then hobbled, I turned the wheel as I slowed, and the stricken vehicle coasted jerkily into the large empty car park of the Road House at Gallows Corner. I jumped out and scrabbled in my doctor's bag in the boot for a torch then surveyed the damage – I had a completely flat tyre. I had never changed a wheel before – how difficult could it be?

I looked around for inspiration– the moon was out, and a few fluffy clouds scudded across the sky. Angus wouldn't be too pleased to be got out of bed on his one night off.

I opened the boot again and lifted all my clutter out onto the tarmac – my doctor's bag and my box of emergency drugs and dressings and the obstetric bag. I then set about lifting the carpeted flap in the floor of the boot and, there was the spare and, yes, this must be a jack. I knelt on the Tarmac and felt for somewhere obvious to fit the jack. I put my head down and peered up into the wheel arch with the torch to discover where to place it – nowhere announced itself.

I needed advice – I really needed to talk to Angus – the side door of the pub was visible and there was a light on upstairs – I knocked – no answer. I knocked again – no answer but another light came on upstairs. I knocked again and could now hear movement behind the closed door. 'Clear off – can't you see we are closed,' said a muffled voice from behind the door.

'Can you help me – I've broken down – I need to phone.'

'We don't open the door at night,' said a woman's voice.

Do not judge this lady too harshly – the evening news had, only a day or two before, reported another victim of the Yorkshire Ripper, whose body had been found only a few miles from the road that ran outside this hostelry, albeit 185 miles further north. The Hadley Herald, which came out that day and whose well-thumbed copy still lay on the bar, had reassured its readers that the local police had been making enquires in the lay-bys and transport cafes up and down the main transport routes as suspicion fell, as it often does, on those men with an excuse for being away from home at night – the long-distance lorry drivers.

I understood her reluctance to open the door. I knelt on the ground and opened the letter box with one hand, 'I'm so sorry – I'm the doctor-on-call for this area – I've got a puncture – can I give you my home number and ask you to call my husband – he'll come and get me.' I tore a prescription from the pad in my pocket and tearing it in half scribbled my telephone number on it and put it into the mouth of the door – it was snatched from the other side – nothing else was said.

I returned to my car and looked around – I was clearly visible from the Hadley Road and also from the dual-carriageway section of the A1. Although it was the main north/south highway there was hardly any traffic – I had better do what I could while I waited (assuming he would get my message). I opened the boot a third time and worked out how to extract the spare wheel – it was much heavier than I imagined. As I was bent double, trying to heave it out, I became aware of a large presence behind me, there was a hiss of air brakes, I stood up banging my head on the lid – a huge lorry had rolled stealthily in behind me and dazzled me with its headlights. I held my hand up to shield my eyes and was aware of movement in the halo of light. A tall, muscular young man entered the cone of light. I could see his long greasy hair as it flopped about his blotchy, stubbled face as he moved restlessly from foot to foot.

'A maiden in distress! Wot you doing out at this time of night?'

'Thank you – I'm fine – I have summoned assistance,' I sounded haughty and defensive. 'My husband is on his way,' I added, smiling weakly and shifting my drug box around the corner of the car with my foot.

'He shouldn't let a tasty little thing like you out alone at night – specially not round here. 'Specially not at the moment.'

He said this as he moved me to one side and pulled the spare wheel clean out of its nest with one huge hand – he held it nonchalantly by his side as he gathered up the jack in his other hand, adding. 'You can shine the torch.'

'Cor! I don't know who tightened these up,' he said straining at the hub nuts, he stopped and went back to his cab and returned wielding an iron bar.

Shit! I thought.

At that moment as the man fitted the hollow iron bar over the handle of the spanner to increase the leverage (that's clever) another lorry drove in off the Hadley Road. It was an old, battered and dented, maroon coal wagon with what looked like scrap metal on the back. It parked with its head lights shining on my vehicle from the other side and from it emerged a scruffy man, lithe, dark haired and bearded. He swung himself down from the cab. 'Can I help with anything?' he said casting an appraising eye around the scene.

'No!' said the incumbent knight errant and, with a crack, the last hub nut yielded.

'Here you are, Mate!' said the other rolling the spare into position. 'Does that need a bit of air? I'll get my pump.'

'Safety in numbers', said my mother from somewhere in my head as I stood back watching the young men as they vied for dominance. What do I do when they've finished the job? I asked... My mother did not answer.

As it happened both young men seemed reluctant to leave me to the mercy of the other, neither was willing to leave first, they both made excuses and hovered about indulging in light-hearted banter. I wondered if I should offer them both payment (not that I had more than a few coins for the phone), should I jump in the car, lock the doors and drive off with a jolly wave – I was penned in by the lorries. Meanwhile they continued to weave around each other showing off. Car lights appeared in the distance – Angus's car drew up.

'Here's my husband, thank you both so much! Thank you for waiting. Angus, these kind gentlemen...'

Angus was looking at the wheels of my car. 'Shame you couldn't let me know you'd sorted it out before I drove all this way...' Then to the men, 'Can I give you chaps something?'

Both were now withdrawing hastily, heading back to their cabs with gracious refusals. The juggernaut hissed and rumbled off, the driver saluting. The coal lorry gave a little choke and a puff of oily exhaust, a toot of the horn, then also headed off into the night.

'I'll see you off then follow you back, not that there is much point, it's nearly time to go to work.'

'Just a minute!'

'What now!' grumbled Angus, I scribbled a note on the other half of the torn prescription and popped it through the letter box of the pub.

'Okay – I'm off!'

As I drove home I became aware for the first time of the two headed creature that I would become as I wondered what had happened to me that night – had I been rescued by two knights of the road (salt of the earth) or had I had a narrow escape. I visualised my half-naked body lying in a ditch my brains smeared on my wet face, the rag that he had wiped the iron bar with thrown down in the wet grass. Had Angus just had a wasted journey, or had he arrived in the nick of time – it just depended on which head I was looking out of – how I saw the world. And all the time the world was changing – I was changing.

It would be fifteen years before I got my first mobile phone, but the following weekend I got my dad to supervise me as I put the wheel with the new tyre back on my car and put the spare back in the boot, thereafter I always carried a strong hollow metal bar down beside my driving seat – for the wheel nuts.

Chapter 29.

Tom

It was as a GP trainee that I had started to discover something magic, a sort of alchemy – it was something that happened in the consulting room when I was alone with a patient. I had perhaps got an inkling of it when I sat quietly in the corner in my teaching practice and spied on the senior partner in consultation with an old familiar patient or when I watched Jaz with a disturbed patient that he could somehow touch with his mind – could contact when others could not. It was a kind of intimacy.

I had tried to explain it once in my seminar group to my fellow trainees who had erupted into hilarity and the supervisor had looked worried and questioned me like a policeman about my use of the word 'intimacy'. I tried to explain that it had nothing to do with sex (more gales of laughter) it was a closeness based on trust and confidentiality, a connectedness, understanding and caring and an acceptance – an openness – a special channel of communication. I looked around the room at the sea of disconnected faces.

'You need to learn to defend yourself!' said one of the others (a thoughtful young man). 'Learn to keep your distance enough to maintain your authority – you'll be up all hours of the day and night and they'll walk all over you if you let them!'

'But if you have a relationship with your patient,' (more laughter). 'With respect and clear boundaries…'

'Good luck with that!' said an ironic voice.

'I think you should be careful with the term 'intimacy' – it tends to mean one thing and one thing only,' said the supervisor.

'Well, I can't think of another word that explains it and I think it is a poor do if 'intimacy' is only allowed to be associated with sex – what sort of society is that!' I said petulantly and with that thought the supervisor drew the session to a close.

But that is what it was – what it would be. I would have hundreds (thousands) of intimate encounters in the confidential, secure confines of a consulting room, or a child's bedroom, or by a deathbed, or during childbirth, or, sometimes, just a glance across a court room or at a funeral. Making deep emotional connections is (that young man was right) a dangerous pursuit – one can feel another's pain but not at the cost of the rational and the analytical. I might find that I can wheedle my way into someone's brain but to effect change (therapy) I have to maintain objectivity so that I can challenge the negative harmful emotions that I find there.

That objectivity is the difference between a friend and a doctor.

As a doctor it is the difference between giving yourself and losing yourself – it was the most important of all the lessons that I would take with me on my journey

I was cutting my parent's front hedge with rather blunt and stiff garden shears. In the next garden Billy, a Polish rheumatologist, was trimming his hedge with an electric cutter. Billy's circumstances had been reduced by a recent divorce which had wrenched him from his old life as an NHS general practitioner and thrown him upon the mercy of the local hospital as a rheumatologist. Being a clever and well qualified physician, he was soon appointed as a consultant, which was why he and his new wife, Anna, now lived in a semi in Hertfordshire – attached to my parents. This recent upturn in his status but downturn in his finances was considerably eased by the discovery of a soul mate in my father, Geoff.

United by a love of salted fish, flavoured vodka and with wartime experiences to share they were to become allies in the struggle with modern life – bureaucracy, flat-pack furniture, D-I-Y and the ascendency of women (not including their medical daughters!)

At this moment Evelyn brought out two mugs of coffee for the workers and Billy switched off his noisy machine. 'How is the General Practice, Daughter of Geoffski?'

'Excellent! Thank you, you can call me Diana. In fact, better than I expected – I started off thinking I'd go back into hospital medicine but I've decided to start looking out for a practice.'

'Here, I hope – Anna would like a nice lady doctor.'

'No, I really want a small rural practice somewhere near Angus's job in the north of the county.'

'No, no, no! My Dear. Small practices are a thing of the past.' He said with authority. 'Everyone is joining up their practices to reduce the night work. The last remaining are one-man practices, and the Health Authority won't give you one of those unless you have a lot of experience and have worked alone for years. They don't like the notion of people pottering along in their own way, insulated from any sort of peer review – they think you might be bumping people off unless you have partners to keep an eye on you. Believe me, I do many domiciliary visits in the area you are talking about.'

'That is exactly what my trainer says but I did spend a few days in Marsh End – three partners and a cottage hospital, where they still do their own deliveries, appendectomies and gall bladders!'

'I know exactly the one you mean – the senior partner was only recently forced by the Health Authority to provide a seat in his room for patients – before that they had to stand to attention – to be fair, he met them face-to-face with their notes on a sort of lectern and him perched on a high stool (like something out of Dickens – it speeded things up no-end.'

'I heard about him. He retired a bit back – I'm sorry I missed him. It's still quite old-fashioned, in that they do everything themselves.'

'You mean modern – that is the way the College would have it.'

'Yes, well I think I would too. Anyway, they have an able-bodied young partner, so they don't need me.'

A fortnight later Billy rang me at home, having extracted my phone number from my father. 'I have someone I would like you to meet! He's a local GP, from the north of the county – very well thought of – very caring – appears every now and again in A&E with a sick patient – in his pyjamas and bedroom slippers. I visited him a few days ago to see a patient with lupus erythematosus which, to his credit, he had already diagnosed even though the lady herself was convinced that she was cursed, but that is another story. His name is Tom Clare and I found him in very low spirits – tired and fed up with the pressure of single-handed practice. What you need, I said, is a nice young partner!'

It was all happening again.

Angus and I stood at the lodge of the large, ugly Victorian house in the middle of the village – the great square edifice was painted blancmange pink. 'It can mean only one of two things,' said Angus. 'He is colour blind or they did it to make it easier to find.'

At the side of the house, we could see a man, a workman in blue overalls and a black beret, he looked like Winston Churchill except that instead of a large cigar he had a pipe which chugged clouds of smoke. Around him was gathered a flock of enthusiastic but disparate fowl – a white goose, a Muscovy duck, several multi-coloured hens and a cockerel that kept jumping into the air and flapping. The biggest Alsatian that I had ever seen lay on the steps leading to the main door of the house. As we walked through the drizzle down the drive towards the group I could feel the smile on my face was getting broader. A procession of grumbling guinea fowl entered the scene from under the branches of the old apple tree, its bows heavy with huge Bramley apples.

'Is that a golden pheasant?' I called as we got within earshot.

'Yes, he's rather fine, isn't he?' said the man. 'You the young doctor?' I nodded.

'Mind that damned cockerel, he's a vicious bastard – you'd better come in... I'm Tom and you must be the surgeon!' he said wiping his hand on his overalls and proffering it to Angus. 'Not so keen on wildlife, eh? Eh?' he said to Angus. 'Shove that dog out of the way so your husband can get in – that's Buster, he's on the payroll – we haven't been broken into yet...'

'I'm not surprised!' said Angus.

'Hello Buster,' I said warmly, holding out my hand for him to sniff. Buster wagged his tail; he knew!